A Reconciliation Sourcebook

The Sourcebook Series:

A Reconciliation Sourcebook

Edited by
Kathleen Hughes
Joseph A. Favazza

Art by
Chuck Ludeke

LITURGY
TRAINING
PUBLICATIONS

Acknowledgments

We are grateful to the many authors and publishers who have given permission to include their work. Every effort has been made to determine the ownership of all texts and to make proper arrangements for their use. Any oversight that may have occurred, if brought to our attention, will gladly be corrected in future editions. The many people who contributed entries for this book are listed in the introduction.

Acknowledgments will be found in the notes. Permission to reprint any texts in this book must be obtained from the copyright owners.

Acquisitions editor: Victoria M. Tufano
Production editor: Audrey Novak Riley
Permissions editor: Theresa Houston
Editorial assistance: Lorraine Schmidt
Production: Lisa Buckley
Production artist: James Mellody-Pizzato
Series design format: Michael Tapia

Printed in the United States of America

A reconciliation sourcebook / edited by Kathleen Hughes,
    Joseph A. Favazza ; art by Chuck Ludeke.
            p.   cm. — (The Sourcebook series)
        ISBN 1-56854-098-1
        1. Penance. 2. Reconciliation — Religious aspects —
    Catholic Church. 3. Catholic Church — Doctrines. 4. Catholic
    Church — Liturgy. I. Hughes, Helen Kathleen. II. Favazza,
    Joseph A., 1954 - . III. Series: Sourcebook series (Liturgy
    Training Publications)
        BX2260.R342 1997
        234'.5 — dc21   97-698
                                                                    CIP

ISBN 1-56854-098-1
RECON

Contents

Introduction

The experience of alienation and reconciliation is so fundamentally human that no one field of study or branch of the humanities can contain it. For this reason, the reader will find in this Reconciliation Sourcebook a wide range of texts that attempt to give insight from a variety of cultural and disciplinary starting points. Even so, the experience escapes us. Deep within us, we know that to be human is to be in communion with others beyond the place where our flesh ends. Yet, even at the same moment of this insight of relational intimacy, we know equally well that our deep desire for communion is never quite realized. Sin, guilt, pain, bondage (just to name a few of the most familiar metaphors for this experience of unrealized intimacy) prevent us from the very thing that drives our lives.

To end here might lead to despair; indeed, history, both personal and public, is full of examples of those who acquiesced to the seductive power of melancholy over the human condition. If these few texts do nothing else, they (re)inspire hope that the work of reconciliation is even more human and thus more fundamental to one's life-project than the brokenness and fragmentation none of us can escape. While from a theological perspective we might call this movement toward reconciliation grace, theology is not the only language spoken in these pages. These texts address alienation at many levels, and just as richly express different languages of reconciliation: forgiveness, healing, liberation, mercy, joyfulness, meaning—the list goes on.

We use the familiar parable of the Prodigal Son (Luke 15:11–24) as the organizing framework for these texts. It is a narrative that highlights the many and necessary exigencies of the process of reconciliation: division, forgetfulness, alienation, honest remembrance, contrition, penance, mercy without condition, ritual, celebration, proclamation. While it has helped us to sort the texts for the purpose of this project, the reader will soon realize that our decision about the placement of a particular text was, in many cases, arbitrary. This is due to two reasons: the richness of many of these texts lends them to the entire process of reconciliation rather than to one moment in the process; and the experience of reconciliation is quite messy and defies logical sequence. Even so, we found this parable to be a workable means to allow these texts to speak for themselves without forcing them against their will to conform to any particular theme.

Our audacious attempts to compile a sourcebook on reconciliation could not have been accomplished without substantial and impressive help. We asked colleagues and friends to contribute selections, and we received generous responses from nearly fifty of them: J. Robert Baker, John J. Begley, SJ, Eleanor Bernstein, CSJ, Barbara E. Bowe, RSCJ, Sheila Browne, RSM, David J. Cinquegrani, CP, Kathleen Cour, OP, James Dennison, Rosemary Dewey, RSCJ, Godfrey Diekmann, OSB, James Donohue, CR, Doris Donnelly, Toinette M. Eugene, Peter C. Finn, Timothy Fitzgerald, Edward Foley, CAPUCHIN, John B. Foley, SJ, Mary Frohlich, Genevieve Glen, OSB, Richard Gula, SS, Sally Harmony, Stephen R. Haynes, J. Frank Henderson, Denise Herrmann, CSA, Barbara Hoffman, Lawrence A. Hoffman, Gabe Huck, Jan Michael Joncas, Sharon Karam, RSCJ, Jeffrey M. Kemper, Robert J. Kennedy, Bruce H. Lescher, Tina Moreau, J-Glenn Murray, SJ, Paul J. Niemann, Melissa Musick Nussbaum, Ronald A. Oakham, OCARM, Timothy E. O'Connell, Carolyn A. Osiek, RSCJ, Gilbert Ostdiek, OFM, Jorge Perales, Paul Philibert, OP, Daniel E. Pilarczyk, Barbara E. Quinn, RSCJ, Jay Cooper Rochelle, Victoria Tufano, Paul J. Wadell, CP, and Joyce Ann Zimmerman, CPPS. Because of their interest, scholarship and commitment, this book contains a much richer variety of selected texts.

While we have strived to select texts across religious traditions and across a variety of genres and disciplines, sometimes our balance is far from perfect. We would like to have included more texts by women. Every reader will wonder how we could have overlooked their favorite text on the topic. While we had to stop somewhere and publish this work, the very genre of a sourcebook means that it is a work in progress. Feel free to add your own texts to the ones we have included here. We have already discovered others we now wish could be included.

We have edited texts to use inclusive language if such editing did not change the meaning of the text. All scripture comes from the New Revised Standard Version which uses inclusive language in its translation whenever possible.

In the end, this sourcebook on reconciliation, like those published before it, is like going to a wine-tasting. For some, it will be enough to sip a little from the full variety of short texts included here and come away satisfied. For others, one text or another may so overwhelm your palate that you will have to buy an entire bottle. For these connoisseurs, the endnotes will prove extraordinarily helpful in locating the full text. In whatever unique way you use this sourcebook, may it help you to drink deeply of and become inebriated with the human drama of alienation and reconciliation. To our minds, becoming human can be accomplished in no less passionate way.

Kathleen Hughes, RSCJ
Joseph A. Favazza

There was a man who had two sons. The younger of them said to his father, "Father, give me my share of the property that will belong to me." So he divided his property between them. A few days later the younger son gathered all he had and traveled to a distant country, and there he squandered his property in dissolute living. When he had spent everything, a severe famine took place throughout that country, and he began to be in need. So he went and hired himself out to one of the citizens of that country, who sent him to his fields to feed the pigs. He would gladly have filled himself with the pods that the pigs were eating; and no one gave him anything. But when he came to himself he said, "How many of my father's hired hands have bread enough and to spare, but here I am dying of hunger! I will get up and go to my father, and I will say to him, 'Father, I have sinned against heaven and before you; I am no longer worthy to be called your son; treat me like one of your hired hands.'" So he set off and went to his father. But while he was still far off, his father saw him and was filled with compassion; he ran and put his arms around him and kissed him. Then the son said "Father, I have sinned against heaven and before you; I am no longer worthy to be called your son." But the father said to his slaves, "Quickly, bring out a robe — the best one — and put it on him; put a ring on his finger and sandals on his feet. And get the fatted calf and kill it, and let us eat and celebrate; for this son of mine was dead and is alive again; he was lost and is found!" And they began to celebrate.

☐

LUKE 15:11–24

THERE WAS A MAN WHO HAD TWO SONS. THE YOUNGER OF THEM SAID TO HIS FATHER, "FATHER, GIVE ME THE SHARE OF THE PROPERTY THAT WILL BELONG TO ME." SO HE DIVIDED HIS PROPERTY BETWEEN THEM.

Luke 15:11 – 12

~

RECENTLY the newspapers carried the story of a man who boarded a bus with the full intention and desire of going to Detroit, but when at the end of a long trip he alighted at the destination, he found himself, not in Detroit, but in Kansas City. He had caught the wrong bus. Something like that goes on habitually in human life. People on the whole desire good things [and] find themselves somewhere else altogether! . . . The Prodigal Son did not start out for a swine pasture.

Harry Emerson Fosdick

WHEN was I ever anything but kind to him?
    But I'll not have the fellow back," he said.
"I told him so last haying, didn't I?
'If he left then,' I said, 'that ended it.'
What good is he? Who else will harbor him
At his age for the little he can do?
What help he is there's no depending on.
Off he goes always when I need him most."

Robert Frost

M ILTON was right," said my teacher. "The choice of every lost soul can be expressed in the words 'Better to reign in hell than serve in heaven.' There is always something they insist on keeping, even at the price of misery. There is always something they prefer to joy — that is, to reality."

C. S. Lewis

O RIGINAL sin is the universal and socialized withdrawal from the mystery of which we yet continue to draw for all our meaning and value. Original sin is the socialized truncation of human life, the systematic reduction of the child of mystery to the banal world of our own making.

Sebastian Moore

I read it in your word, and learn it from
the history of the gestures of your warm
wise hands, rounding themselves to form
and circumscribe the shapes that are to come.
Aloud you said: to live, and low: to die,
and you repeated, tirelessly: to be.
And yet there was no death till murder came.
Then through your perfect circles ran a rent
and a cry tore,
scattering the voices that not long before
had gently blent
to utter you,
to carry you,
bridge across the abyss—

And what they since have stammered
are the fragments only
of your old name.

Rainer Maria Rilke

HE did not even look pleased to have saved me. I would confess that it had been eleven years since I had been to confession. I would confess my three lovers. But my worst sin I would not confess, for the church had not thought of a confessable name for it: the hunger of my spirit, the utter selfishness of my heart. But I had devised my own repentance: I was here. It was a penance more difficult than the church could have imagined exacting, and because of this the church could never be of comfort to me. I would pay for my greed with my future. I had thought myself at the center of my own life, the universe, and for this error I would give my life. Christ was right; he had said, "You must lose your life in order to gain it." By insisting on my own life I was in danger of losing everything.   Mary Gordon

THE men and women in the Bible are sinners like ourselves, but there is one sin they do not commit, our arch-sin: they do not dare confine God to a circumscribed space or division of life, "religion." They have not the insolence to draw boundaries around God's commandments and say: "Up to this point you are sovereign, but beyond these bounds begins the sovereignty of science or society or the state."   Martin Buber

No man is an island, entire of itself; every man is a piece of the continent, a part of the mainland. If a clod be washed away by the sea, Europe is the less, as well as if a promontory were, as well as if a manor of thy friends or of thine own were. Any man's death diminishes me, because I am involved in mankind. And therefore never send to know for whom the bell tolls. It tolls for thee.

John Donne
Seventeenth century

THERE is no sin, not even the most intimate and secret one, the most strictly individual one, that exclusively concerns the person committing it. With greater or lesser violence, with greater or lesser harm, every sin has repercussions on the . . . whole human family.

Pope John Paul II

THERE can be no reconciliation until there is recognition of need, of rupture, of alienation, of sin, of being drawn to conversion and a new life. If you are a member of the perfect society you have no need of conversion and little need for adequate rituals to express healing. Who needs healing if you aren't broken? How difficult it is to experience conversion when numbers of people feel they do not need it. How difficult it is to stand in need of the mercy of God if some in the community think they are able to define it and mete it out. Reconciliation cannot happen in a community where the majority believe that they don't need it and that the minority don't deserve it. Shunning follows logically from such a posture.

Kathleen Hughes

A moral principle in the little Amish community is the practice of *Bann und Meidung.* These words rendered in English mean excommunication and shunning. . . . Joseph was excommunicated with the counsel of the assembly and was informed in their presence. After being asked to leave the service he thought to himself: "It is strange to think that I am now to be 'mited.' I don't feel very comfortable." At home, the young man was shunned: he could no longer eat at the family table. He ate at a separate table, with the young children, or after the baptized persons were finished eating. Joseph was urged to mend his ways, to make good his broken promise. His normal work relations and conversational pattern were strained. Several times he attended preaching services with his family. Since members may not accept services, goods, or favors from excommunicated members, he could not take his sisters to church, even if he used a buggy instead of his offensive automobile, but they could drive a buggy and take him along. It was not long until Joseph accepted employment with a non-Amish person and began using his automobile for transportation to and from home. When shunned friends came to his home for conversation, Joseph's parents met them at the gate and turned them away. It was not long until father and mother asked him to leave home. He explained: "I had to move away from home or my parents could not take communion. My parents were afraid that younger persons in the family would be led astray. The didn't exactly chase me off the place, but I was no longer welcome at home."

John A. Hostetler

Trees by their yield
Are known; but I —
My sap is sealed,
My root is dry.
If life within
I none can shew
(Except for sin),
Nor fruit above, —
It must be so —
I do not love.

Will no one show
I argued ill?
Because, although
Self-sentenced, still
I keep my trust.
If he would prove
And search me through
Would he not find
(What yet there must
Be hid behind

Gerard Manley
Hopkins

Nineteenth century

THE Buddha taught his students to develop a power of love so strong that their minds become like a pure, flowing river that cannot be burned. No matter what kind of material is thrown into it, it will not burn. Many experiences — good, bad, and indifferent — are thrown into the flowing river of our lives, but we are not burned, owing to the power of the love in our hearts.

The concepts of separateness that have dominated our lives have produced tremendous suffering. What we have taken to be real is in fact a hallucination. The division between self and other is the degradation of our highest human potential: the liberation of the mind that is love. The critical moment of the path, which breaks open the loving heart, is the realization that we have never existed as separate, isolated beings. When wisdom recognizes our oneness and sees the interconnectedness of all beings, it fills us with a degree of happiness that transforms our lives.

Sharon Salzberg

WHO will separate us from the love of Christ? Will hardship, or distress, or persecution, or famine, or nakedness, or peril, or sword? As it is written,

"For your sake we are being killed all day long:
   we are accounted as sheep to be slaughtered."

No, in all these things we are more than conquerors through him who loved us. For I am convinced that neither death, nor life, nor angels, nor rulers, nor things present, nor things to come, nor powers, nor height, nor depth, nor anything else in all creation, will be able to separate us from the love of God in Christ Jesus our Lord.

Romans 8:35–39

LET us intercede for those who are involved in some transgression, that forbearance and humility may be given them, so that they may submit, not to us but to the will of God. For in this way the merciful remembrance of them in the presence of God and all the saints will be fruitful and perfect for them. Let us accept correction, which no one ought to resent, dear friends. The reproof which we give one to another is good and exceedingly useful, for it unites us with the will of God. For thus says the Holy Word: "The Lord has indeed disciplined me, but has not handed me over to death."

Clement of Rome
Second century

EACH of you, a bordered country,
Delicate and strangely made proud,
Yet thrusting perpetually under siege.
Your armed struggles for profit
Have left collars of waste upon
My shore, currents of debris upon my breast.
Yet today I call you to my riverside,
If you will study war no more.

Maya Angelou

FOR in every choice we made in the past, we appropriated that moment of the past into ourselves forever. Choice is therefore always both irrevocable and unretractable, even though it is in some sense revisable. In every choice I engrave something in myself in a definitive way. We must not stop short of saying that I will never be without this choice. I am bound to it for as long as I exist as myself, even if that happens to be for all eternity; I am this choice, from now on. In the future I can choose to revise it but not in the sense of going back to who I was before I made it. I will never be able to be anything more than an act of contrition for the evil I have appropriated into myself.

Jerome A. Miller

Of all qualities, sadness is the worst. It is the attribute of the incurable egotist, who is always thinking: "This should have been mine; I have been wrongfully deprived of that." It is always *I*.

Chenoch of Alexander
Nineteenth century

Lady of silences
Calm and distressed
Torn and most whole
Rose of memory
Rose of forgetfulness
Exhausted and life-giving
Worried reposeful
The single Rose
Is now the Garden
Where all loves end
Terminate torment
Of love unsatisfied
The greater torment
Of love satisfied
End of the endless
Journey to no end
Conclusion of all that
Is inconclusible
Speech without word and
Word of no speech
Grace to the Mother
For the Garden
Where all love ends.

T. S. Eliot

SOMETHING there is that doesn't love a wall,
That sends the frozen-ground-swell under it,
And spills the upper boulders in the sun;
And makes gaps even two can pass abreast.
The work of hunters is another thing:
I have come after them and made repair
Where they have left not one stone on a stone,
But they would have the rabbit out of hiding,
To please the yelping dogs. The gaps I mean,
No one has seen them made or heard them made,
But at spring mending-time we find them there.
I let my neighbor know beyond the hill;
And on a day we meet to walk the line
And set the wall between us once again.
We keep the wall between us as we go.
To each the boulders that have fallen to each.
And some are loaves and some so nearly balls
We have to use a spell to make them balance:
"Stay where you are until our backs are turned!"
We wear our fingers rough with handling them.

Oh, just another kind of outdoor game,
One on a side. It comes to little more:
There where it is we do not need the wall:
He is all pine and I am apple orchard.
My apple trees will never get across
And eat the cones under his pines, I tell him
He only says, "Good fences make good neighbors."
Spring is the mischief in me, and I wonder
If I could put a notion in his head:
"*Why* do they make good neighbors? Isn't it
Where there are cows? But here there are no cows.
Before I built a wall I'd ask to know
What I was walling in or walling out,
And to whom I was like to give offense.
Something there is that doesn't love a wall,
That wants it down." I could say "Elves" to him,
But it's not elves exactly, and I'd rather
He said it for himself. I see him there
Bringing a stone grasped firmly by the top
In each hand, like an old-stone savage armed.
He moves in darkness as it seems to me,
Not of woods only and the shade of trees
He will not go behind his father's saying,
And he likes having thought of it so well
He says again, "Good fences make good neighbors."   Robert Frost

B E gracious to all that are near and dear to me, and keep
us all in thy fear and love. Guide us, good Lord, and
govern us by the same Spirit, that we may be so united to
thee here as not to be divided when thou art pleased to call
us hence, but may together enter into thy glory, through   John Wesley
Jesus Christ, our blessed Lord and Saviour.   Eighteenth century

THEN the LORD God said, "See, the man has become like one of us, knowing good and evil; and now, he might reach out his hand and take also from the tree of life, and eat, and live forever" — therefore the LORD God sent him forth from the garden of Eden, to till the ground from which he was taken. He drove out the man; and at the east of the garden of Eden he placed the cherubim, and a sword flaming and turning to guard the way to the tree of life.

Genesis 3:22 – 24

A certain Timothy, a hermit, heard of a certain heedless brother: and when his abbot asked him what should be done with him, gave his counsel to cast him out from the monastery. Now after he had been cast out, temptation came to Timothy: and when he was confessing in the presence of God and saying, "Have mercy upon me," there came to him a voice saying, "Timothy, this tribulation came to thee for this one thing, that thou hast despised thy brother in the time of his temptation."

Sayings of the Desert Fathers

HUMAN beings, therefore are divided interiorly. As a result, the entire life of women and men, both individual and social, shows itself to be a struggle, and a dramatic one, between good and evil, between light and darkness. People find that they are unable of themselves to overcome the assaults of evil successfully, so that everyone feels as if in chains.

Pastoral Constitution on the Church in the Modern World

So, there is a strange paradox here: that "sin," which is usually considered a very negative word, is in actuality a word which implies an affirmation of faith. It is a way of acknowledging, first, that God exists and, second, that there is some discrepancy between how things are and how we think God wants them, between the world of the real and the world of the faith-inspired ideal, between human behavior and the content of the religious challenge for life.

Timothy E. O'Connell

You, neighbor God, if sometimes in the night
I rouse you with loud knocking, I do so
only because I seldom hear you breathe
and know: you are alone.
And should you need a drink, no one is there
to reach it to you, groping in the dark.
Always I hearken. Give but a small sign.
I am quite near.

Between us there is but a narrow wall,
and by sheer chance; for it would take
merely a call from your lips or from mine
to break it down,
and that without a sound.

The wall is built of your images.

They stand before you hiding you like names,
And when the light within me blazes high
that in my inmost soul I know you by,
the radiance is squandered on their frames.

And then my senses, which too soon grow lame,
exiled from you, must go their homeless ways.

Rainer Maria Rilke

SOMEWHERE in between my baptism
      and my daily life
My power like unto God's became scattered
I forgot my original union with God.
And as I grew
I chose
     good and evil
     light and darkness
     life and death
     grace and sin.

With my baptism lost

I began to live my life fragmented,
standing on the edge of my baptismal powers
Macrina Wiederkehr   blind to their presence in the depths of my soul.

THE formidable power that forgiveness exercises in our
lives enables us to acknowledge that the decisions of
human life, even when they turn out badly, are not above
Doris Donnelly   repair.

ALMIGHTY and merciful God,
you have brought us together in the name of your Son
to receive your mercy and grace in our time of need.
Open our eyes to see the evil we have done.
Touch our hearts and convert us to yourself.

Where sin has divided and scattered,
may your love make one again;
where sin has brought weakness,
may your power heal and strengthen;
where sin has brought death,
Rite of penance   may your Spirit raise to new life.

L ET us pray,
for all those who are in great difficulty—
for those who have lost their faith
in humanity and love, their faith in God,
for those who seek truth but cannot find it.
Let us pray for all married people
who have drifted apart from each other
and for all priests who have broken down
under the strain of their office. . . .

Let us pray
for the town we live and work in,
for all the people in it who are lonely,
for those whose voices are never heard
and those who find no friends.
Let us pray
for the homeless and those without shelter
and for all who are disheartened
and feel that they have been betrayed. . . .

Let us ask the Lord for forgiveness
for the suffering that we cause to others,
for our forgetfulness and neglect of others,
for our lack of understanding for each other,
for speaking ill of other people
and for the bitterness and spite
we so often feel toward others,
for not being able to forgive.

*A Christian's Prayer
Book*

A FEW DAYS LATER THE YOUNGER SON GATHERED ALL HE HAD AND TRAVELED TO A DISTANT COUNTRY, AND THERE HE SQUANDERED HIS PROPERTY IN DISSOLUTE LIVING.   Luke 15:13

~

THERE are only two kinds of people in the end: those who say to God, "Thy will be done," and those to whom God says, "*Thy* will be done." All that are in hell, choose it. Without that self-choice there could be no hell.

C. S. Lewis

ONCE upon a time there was a peasant woman and a very wicked woman she was. And she died and did not leave a single good deed behind. The devils caught her and plunged her into a lake of fire. So her guardian angel stood and wondered what good deed of hers he could remember to tell to God. "She once pulled up an onion in her garden," said he, "and gave it to a beggar woman." And God answered: "You take that onion then, hold it out to her in the lake, and let her take hold of it and be pulled out. And if you can pull her out of the lake, let her come to Paradise, but if the onion breaks, then the woman must stay where she is." The angel ran to the woman and held out the onion to her. "Come," said he, "catch hold and I'll pull you out." And he began cautiously pulling her out. He had just about pulled her out, when the other sinners in the lake, seeing how she was being drawn out, caught hold of her so as to be pulled out with her. But she was a very wicked woman and she began kicking them off. "I'm to be pulled out, not you. It's my onion, not yours." As soon as she said that, the onion broke. And she fell back into the lake and she is burning there to this day. So her guardian angel wept and went away.

Fyodor Dostoyevsky
Nineteenth century

S AY to them, As I live, says the Lord GOD, I have no plea-
sure in the death of the wicked, but that the wicked turn
from their ways and live; turn back, turn back from your
evil ways; for why will you die, O house of Israel?   Ezekiel 33:11

W HEN the sins of our fathers visit us
We do not have to play host.
We can banish them with forgiveness
As God, in God's largeness and laws.   August Wilson

H AVE mercy, tender God,
forget that I defied you.
Wash away my sin,
cleanse me from my guilt.

I know my evil well,
it stares me in the face,
evil done to you alone
before your very eyes.

How right your condemnation!
Your verdict clearly just.
You see me for what I am,
a sinner before my birth.   Psalm 51:3–7

THERE is
a long-suffering lady
with thin hands
who stands on the corner
of Delphia and Lawrence
and forgives you.

"You are forgiven,"
she smiles.

The neighborhood is embarrassed.
It is sure
it has done nothing wrong
yet everyday
in a small voice
it is forgiven.

On the way to the Jewel Food Store
housewives pass her
with hard looks
then whisper
in the cereal section.

Stan Dumke asked her
right out
what she was up to
and
she forgave him.

A group
who care about the neighborhood
agree that if she was old
it would be harmless
or if she was religious
it would be understandable
but as it is . . .
They asked her to move on.

Like all things
with eternal purposes
she stayed.
And she
was informed
upon.

On a most unforgiving day
of snow and slush
while she was reconciling
a reluctant passerby
the State People,
whose business is sanity,
persuaded her into a car.

She is gone.
We are reduced
to forgetting.

John Shea

ɪꜰ there were a balm in Gilead, I would go
To Gilead for your wounds, unhappy land,
Gather you balsam there, and with this hand,
Made deft by pity, cleanse and bind and sew
And drench with healing, that your strength might grow,
(Though love be outlawed, kindness contraband)
And you, O proud and felled, again might stand;
But where to look for balm, I do not know.
The oils and herbs of mercy are so few;
Honour's for sale; allegiance has its price;
The barking of a fox has bought us all;
We save our skins a craven hour or two. —
While Peter warms him in the servants' hall
The thorns are platted and the cock crows twice.

*Edna St. Vincent
Millay*

A brother asked the abbot Pastor, saying, "Trouble has come upon me and I would fain leave this place." And the old man said to him, "For what reason?" And he said, "I have heard tales of a certain brother that do not edify me." And the old man said, "Are the tales true that you have heard?" And he said, "Yes, Father, they are true: for the brother who told me is faithful." And he answering said, "He is not faithful that told you: for if he were faithful, he would never tell you such things: God heard tell of the people of Sodom, but he believed it not till he went down and saw with his own eyes." But he said, "And I have seen with my own eyes." The old man heard him and looked upon the ground and picked up a little straw and said to him, "What is this?" And he answered, "A straw." And again the old man gazed at the roof of the cell and said, "What is this?" And he said, "It is the beam that holds up the room." And the old man said to him, "Take it to heart that your sins are as this beam: the sins of that brother of whom you speak are as this poor straw."

*Sayings of the
The Desert Fathers*

I F we say that we have no sin, we deceive ourselves, and
the truth is not in us. If we confess our sins, he who is faithful and just will forgive us our sins and cleanse us from all
unrighteousness. If we say that we have not sinned, we
make him a liar, and his word is not in us.

My little children, I am writing these things to you so that
you may not sin. But if anyone does sin, we have an advo-
cate with the Father, Jesus Christ the righteous; and he is
the atoning sacrifice for our sins, and not for ours only but
also for the sins of the whole world.   1 John 1:8 — 2:2

F ATHER of mercies
  and God of all consolation,
you do not wish the sinner to die
but to be converted and live.
Come to the aid of your people,
that they may turn from their sins
and live for you alone.
May we be attentive to your word,
confess our sins, receive your forgiveness,
and be always grateful for your loving kindness.
Help us to live the truth in love
and grow into the fullness of Christ, your Son,
who lives and reigns for ever and ever.
Amen.   Rite of penance

L ove is not concerned
with whom you pray
or where you slept
the night you ran away
from home
love is concerned
that the beating of your heart
should kill no one.

Alice Walker

I n a divinized person the godly characteristic is humility, deep in a person's being. Where there is no humility we cannot speak of a divinized person. Christ taught this in words, works and life.

Humility stems from the inner recognition made in the true light that being, life, knowledge, wisdom and power are truly rooted in God, not in the created world. The creature is of itself and has from itself nothing. When it turns away from the true goodness in will and work, nothing is left but wickedness.

Martin Luther
Sixteenth century

WHERE can I hide from you?
How can I escape your presence?
I scale the heavens, you are there!
I plunge to the depths, you are there!

If I fly toward the dawn,
or settle across the sea,
even there you take hold of me,
your right hand directs me.

If I think night will hide me
and darkness give me cover,
I find darkness is not dark.
For you night shines like day,
darkness and light are one.   Psalm 139:7–12

HUMAN society, particularly in the West, is burdened by
a history of infidelity and crime that are enormous,
and all we do is excuse and palliate our falsity, trying to
blame someone else who is as guilty as we are. We are all
guilty, but that means that we must in a very special way
avoid the final guilt of violence or of despair.

Thomas Merton

THIS is the definition of sin: the misuse of powers given   Basil the Great
us by God for doing good.   Fourth century

You don't get to choose how you are going to die. Or when. You can only decide how you're going to live. Now.

Joan Baez

One of the most disturbing facts that came out in the Eichmann trial was that a psychiatrist examined him and pronounced him perfectly sane. I do not doubt it at all, and that is precisely why I find it disturbing.

Thomas Merton

Sin whispers with the wicked,
shares its evil, heart to heart.
These sinners shut their eyes
to all fear of God.
They refuse to see their sin,
to know it and hate it.

Their words ring false and empty,
their plans neglect what is good.
They daydream of evil,
plot their crooked ways
seizing on all that is vile.

Psalm 36:2 – 5

S IN is an unused, unfashionable word, but the facts of life (including my own life) as I look at them — the betrayals, the forgetfulness, the selfishness, the egocentricity — are but the history of humankind written small. There is only one answer to such a vision: It must be accepted. I must simply turn it over to nothing short of grace.

This exposure of ever-deepening congruity between the mad parables of Jesus, the craziness of the gospel, the incomprehensibility of judgment and grace is the only pattern that seems not to anesthetize, not to cosmetize, the human reality. It seems the only pattern big enough to disclose the raw skeleton of human experience. I cannot prove the truth of the Christian faith, but I cannot escape the haunting congruity between the doctrine of God and grace and love and sin and judgment. The more absurd the human drama becomes, the more appropriate the divine drama discloses itself to be.

Joseph Sittler

O thou great Chief, light a candle in my heart, that I may see what is therein, and sweep the rubbish from thy dwelling place.

African schoolgirl's
prayer

I 'LL go no more:
I am afraid to think what I have done;
Look on 't again I dare not.

William Shakespeare
Seventeenth century

No matter how far we have wandered, no matter how much damage we have inflicted on ourselves, God still loves us and still wants what is good for us. That's why God continues to pester us with discontent and uncertainty when we do wrong. That's why God never lets us be fulfilled by anything other than God. That's why God continues to offer us forgiveness.

Daniel E. Pilarczyk

In the end, the deepest question each of us adults faces is the question of where we will point our lives, the question of direction. In some sense everything else leads up to this and is important because of how it relates to this. Sin as a direction-possibility and its blessed alternative of a direction pointed toward God: These alternatives are, in the end, what life is all about.

Timothy E. O'Connell

YOU are the devil," William said then.

Jorge seemed not to understand. If he had been able to see, I would say he stared at his interlocutor with a dazed look. "I?" he said.

"Yes. They lied to you. The devil is not the Prince of Matter; the Devil is the arrogance of the spirit, faith without smile, truth that is never seized by doubt. The Devil is grim because he knows where he is going, and, in moving, he always returns whence he came. You are the Devil, and like the Devil you live in darkness."

Umberto Eco

I am not a mystic and I do not lead a holy life. Not that I can claim any interesting or pleasurable sins (my sense of the devil is strong) but I know all about the garden variety, pride, gluttony, envy and sloth, and what is more to the point, my virtues are as timid as my vices. I think sin occasionally brings one closer to God, but not habitual sin and not this petty kind that blocks every small good. A working knowledge of the devil can be very well had from resisting him.

Flannery O'Connor

S ATAN is a name we use
for darkness in the world,
a goat on which we load
our most horrific sins,
to carry off our guilt.
But all the evil I have seen
was done by human beings.
It isn't a dark angel
who rigs a car into a bomb,
or steals money meant for others' food.
And it wasn't any alien spirit
that chained me to this wall.
One of those who kidnapped me
said once: "No man believes he's evil."
A penetrating and subtle thought
in these circumstances, and from him.
And that's the mystery:
He's not stupid, and doesn't seem insane.
He knows I've done no harm to him or his.
He's looked into my face
each day for years, and
heard me crying in the night.
Still he daily checks my chain,
makes sure my blindfold is secure,
then kneels outside my cell

Terry Anderson   and prays to Allah, merciful, compassionate.

EVEN if there is grave sin that you cannot wash away
yourself with the tears of your repentance, on your
behalf this mother, the church, weeps, she intervenes for
each of her children as a widowed mother for her only
child; for she sympathizes through spiritual suffering when
she sees her children pushed toward death by deadly vices.

Ambrose of Milan
Fourth century

SIN is present in all human life, though not always to
the same degree. Perhaps then human relations can only
come right when we have all come to a right relation
to God.

John Macquarrie

PEOPLE the world over are sick of individualism, of being
sundered from others, of the tragic loss which comes
from thinking and acting alone. They are sick of individualistic, subjective piety because it lacks depth and vision.
They are sick of the individualism that has undone so many
homes. . . . People are sick of the individualism that has
made of political life an unspeakably sordid thing; sick of
the stinking individualism in our economic life that has
denied to workers their rightful place in industrial life; sick,
above all, of the individualism in international life that has
left the world a shambles and now thwarts the efforts to
build a peace. The world is sick of individualism and must
get over it.

Reynold Hillenbrand

A ʟʟ have sinned and come short of the glory of God.
(Paul to the Romans)

The hatred which divides nation from nation, race from
race, class from class.

FATHER FORGIVE

The covetous desires of men and nations to possess what
is not theirs.

FATHER FORGIVE

The greed which exploits the labors of men and lays
waste the earth.

FATHER FORGIVE

Our envy of the welfare and happiness of others.

FATHER FORGIVE

Our indifference to the plight of the homeless and
the refugee.

FATHER FORGIVE

The lust which uses for ignoble ends the bodies of
men and women.

FATHER FORGIVE

The pride which leads us to trust in ourselves and not
in God.

FATHER FORGIVE

Be kind to one another, tender hearted, forgiving one
another, as God in Christ forgave you.
(Paul to the Ephesians)

Plaque in the ruins of
Coventry Cathedral

To stand in the ruins of the old Coventry Cathedral is to stand in one of the most evocative places in England. For people from all over the world, the remains of that building, its noble tower and spire still standing proud on the skyline of a modern industrial city, are an unforgettably poignant reminder of our human condition. They speak not only of what the poet Wilfred Owen called "the pity of war," but also of the inescapable issues that face us all as individual men and women or as peoples and communities. They speak of life, of death, of destiny. The ruins, open to the sky, are like a place of martyrdom—to quote Nikolaus Pevsner, a place in which to ponder life's ultimate questions.

But alongside, its great porch overarching, embracing almost, the place of destruction, rises the new building. And as we are drawn toward it, we begin to grasp the fact that these are not two cathedrals but one, a single statement of faith in the gospel story of death and resurrection. That is why the proper place to begin a visit to Coventry Cathedral is in the ruins, for they are an anteroom to the splendor of the new cathedral as surely as Good Friday prepares for Easter. Coventry Cathedral stands as a sign that this movement from Good Friday to Easter embraces all of human life. It is an icon of a suffering God, through whose death and resurrection come life, light and love.   Michael Sadgrove

WHEN HE HAD SPENT EVERYTHING, A SEVERE FAMINE TOOK
PLACE THROUGHOUT THAT COUNTRY, AND HE BEGAN TO BE IN
NEED. SO HE WENT AND HIRED HIMSELF OUT TO ONE OF THE
CITIZENS OF THAT COUNTRY, WHO SENT HIM TO HIS FIELDS TO
FEED THE PIGS. HE WOULD GLADLY HAVE FILLED HIMSELF WITH
THE PODS THAT THE PIGS WERE EATING; AND NO ONE GAVE
HIM ANYTHING.   Luke 15:14–16

~

WE raise de wheat,
    Dey gib us de corn.
We bake de bread,
Dey gib us de crust.
We sif de meal,
Dey gib us de huss.
We peel de meat,
Dey gib us de skin.
And dat's de way
Dey take us in;
We skim de pot,
Dey gib us de liquor,
And say dat's good enough for nigger.

Frederick Douglass
Nineteenth century

H E was a bad Catholic."

"That's the silliest phrase in common use," Father Rank said.

"And at the end, this — horror. He must have known that he was damning himself."

"Yes, he knew that all right. He never had any trust in mercy — except for other people."

"It's no good even praying . . ."

Father Rank clapped the cover of the diary to and said, furiously, "For goodness sake, Mrs. Scobie, don't imagine you — or I — know a thing about God's mercy."

"The church says . . ."

"I know the church says. The church knows all the rules. But it doesn't know what goes on in a single human heart."   Graham Greene

My face is Mrs. Heyward's,
Long and thin. In the photograph I have of her
She is sending a son
To the Great War. Her mother,
A mill-owner's daughter from Manchester,
Was disowned for running to America
With a Methodist.

I wear Mrs. Hutton's wedding ring:
It's washed countless dishes
At church suppers,
And pulled white shirts
Through a steam-hot wringer.
I have her daughter's fine bones,
My grandmother Totten.
But I'll be stooped like grandmother Norris
When I'm old, with alert eyes:
And while I may never have her faith in Jesus,
At the end, like her,
I know I'll expect to see my mother.

I have no photograph
Of the milliner, a second cousin
Who wed a doctor
Against advice.
She ran away, and the police found her
In Chicago:
She'd bought netting and feathers,
But couldn't remember her name.

Or the girl raped at Bible Camp
By an old preacher, who spoke gently
As he lifted her skirts
And slid his hands
Up her ten-year-old legs.
She sailed for Africa, and mission work,
When I was a child.

I have a scratched recording
Of another aunt, singing hymns
In a rich soprano.
She heard the voices
Of the lost tribes of Israel,
But her own voice led her
Into temptation, and she seduced
A farm boy from the church choir.

She jumped out a window
At the state hospital
The year I was born,
And I want more than anything
To know she has been forgiven.

Kathleen Norris

I would like to live differently from the way I now live. I would like not to cheat people in other countries when I buy bananas by defrauding them of their wages. I would like not to steal when I drink coffee. I do not want to belong to this band of murderers and thieves that our economy represents. I do not want hunger to continue forever. I do not want to live in a system that has proven itself unable to alter hunger in the last thirty years, a system that has not really worked on this problem anywhere in the world, but instead makes weapons, weapons, weapons. I am not free as long as I live in these conditions.

One understands the real social movements in our world, the movements for more justice, more peace, and the integrity of creation, only when one understands them as longings for freedom. Where the Spirit of Christ is, there is freedom. There is liberation for all people, not only for us. Where do we find this Spirit in our world — in our part of the calm, sated, so-called peaceful free world? I will not give an answer here to this question; you have to find the answer yourself. There is no other way.

Dorothee Soelle

LONG ago, Plotinus wrote, "If we are in unity with the Spirit, we are in unity with each other, and so we are all one." . . . When I have lost harmony with another, my whole life is thrown out of tune. God tends to be remote and far away when a desert and sea appear between me and another. I draw close to God as I draw close to my fellows. The great incentive remains ever alert; I cannot be at peace without God, and I cannot be truly aware of God if I am not at peace with my fellows. For the sake of my unity with God, I keep working on my relations with my fellows. This is ever the insistence of all ethical religions.   Howard Thurman

SOME say the world will end in fire,
Some say in ice.
From what I've tasted of desire
I hold with those who favor fire.
But if it had to perish twice,
I think I know enough of hate
To say that for destruction ice
Is also great
And would suffice.   Robert Frost

Your father was only a man who didn't know how to help himself and didn't know better. I kept it from you both because I didn't want you to hate him more than you did. You couldn't know how it was, because he loved Gerald the way he loved both of you, and he picked him up the way he'd picked you up a thousand times. Only this time the diaper wasn't pinned right, and that was my fault, and Gerald slipped out of it, and your father stood there with the diaper in his hand, and Gerald was already dead with a broken neck, I'm sure of that, the way his little head was. I'm sure he never suffered more than a pinprick of pain and then he went to heaven because he was baptized, and I thanked God for that in the same minute I knew he was gone. Your father knelt over him and tried to pick him up, but I said, Don't, it might be his back and we shouldn't move him, and we both knelt there looking at him and trying to see if he was breathing, and finally we both knew he wasn't, and your father fell over on the floor and cried, oh, how he cried, how that man cried. And I cried for him as well as for Gerald, because I knew he'd never get over this as long as he lived. Gerald was gone but your father would have to live with it, and so we held one another and in a minute or so I covered him with a blanket and went up the street for Doctor Lynch and told him I put him on the table to change his diaper and then he rolled off and I never knew he could move so much. He believed me and put accidental death on the record, and it surely was that, even though your father was drinking when it happened, which I know is the reason he went away. But he wasn't drunk the way he got to be in the days after that, when he never saw a sober minute. He had just come home after the car barns and a few jars at the saloon, and he wasn't no different from the way he was a thousand other nights, except what he did was different, and that made him a dead man his whole life. He's the one now that's got to forgive himself, not me, not us.

William Kennedy

I lost my soul in a fit of temper
I threw it at somebody's head
and slammed out
without a second thought

Then I dumped it in a wastebin
along with a love I said I was finished with

I sandpapered my spirit
with a million
bitter barbs
and sent it into orbit
and substituted
guilt instead

My soul went cold
with memories of old friends and kin
who never expected
to be neglected,
and resolutions
I'd eluded

Then one day
I went to feed it
and it was gone
and now I hear it howling
in the wind outside
in the nights
in the hills

and I get the chills inside

and hide
in something that's not important
and it's four in the morning
before I can get warm enough
to weep enough
to fall asleep

Sandy McIntosh

WHEN they had kindled a fire in the middle of the courtyard and sat down together, Peter sat among them. Then a servant-girl, seeing him in the firelight, stared at him and said, "This man also was with him." But he denied it, saying, "Woman, I do not know him." A little later someone else, on seeing him, said, "You also are one of them!" But Peter said, "Man, I am not!" Then about an hour later still another kept insisting, "Surely this man also was with him; for he is a Galilean." But Peter said, "Man, I do not know what you are talking about!" At that moment, while he was still speaking, the cock crowed. The Lord turned and looked at Peter. Then Peter remembered the word of the Lord, how he had said to him, "Before the cock crows today, you will deny me three times." And he went out and wept bitterly.

Luke 22:55–62

FOUL whisp'rings are abroad: unnatural deeds
Do breed unnatural troubles: infected minds
To their deaf pillows will discharge their secrets:
More needs she the divine than the physician.
God, God forgive us all! Look after her;
Remove from her the means of all annoyance,
And still keep eyes upon her. So, good night:
My mind she has mated, and amaz'd my sight.
I think, but dare not speak.

William Shakespeare
Seventeenth century

ETHAN went away to camp when he was twelve — a year ago, almost exactly. Most boys started earlier, but Macon had kept delaying it. Why have a child at all, he asked Sarah, if you were going to ship him off to some godforsaken spot in Virginia? By the time he finally gave in, Ethan was in the top age group — a tall blond sprout of a boy with an open, friendly face and an endearing habit of bouncing on the balls of his feet when he was nervous.

Don't think about it.

He was murdered in a Burger Bonanza his second night at camp. It was one of those deaths that make no sense — the kind where the holdup man has collected his money and is free to go but decides, instead, first to shoot each and every person through the back of the skull.

Ethan wasn't even supposed to be there. He had snuck away from camp with a cabinmate, who waited outside as a lookout.

Blame the camp for not supervising. Blame Burger Bonanza for poor security. Blame the cabinmate for not going in too and altering, perhaps, what took place. (Lookout for what, for God's sake?) Blame Sarah for allowing Ethan to leave home; blame Macon for agreeing; blame even (hell, yes) Ethan for wanting to attend that camp and for sneaking off from it, and for entering Burger Bonanza like some headstrong fool while a holdup was in progress. Blame him for so meekly moving to the kitchen with the others, for placing his hands flat against the wall as he was ordered and no doubt bouncing slightly on the balls of his feet . . .

Don't think about it.   Anne Tyler

GOD, my God,
why have you abandoned me —
far from my cry, my words of pain?
I call by day, you do not answer;
Psalm 22:1 – 2   I call by night, but find no rest.

PUT aside your hatred and animosity. Take pains to
refrain from sharp words. If they escape your lips, do
not be ashamed to let your lips produce the remedy, since
they have caused the wounds. Pardon one another so that
later on you will not remember the injury. The recollection
of an injury is itself wrong. It adds to our anger, nurtures our
sin and hates what is good. It is a rusty arrow and poison
for the soul. It puts all virtue to flight. It is like a worm in
the mind: It confuses our speech and tears to shreds our
petitions to God. It is foreign to charity: It remains planted
Francis of Paola   in the soul like a nail. It is wickedness that never sleeps, sin
Fifteenth century   that never fails. It is indeed a daily death.

YOUNG man —
Young man —
James Weldon   Your arm's too short to box with God.
Johnson

Accuse yourself of your sins before God, who numbers all your ways and anticipates and understands all the thoughts of your mind, and God will forgive the impiety of your heart and lead you from the depths of distress; and if you cry to God from the dust, God will set your foot on a rock and place in your mouth a new song to confess the holy name. For God healed the dull faults of the Ninevites by their triple confession of penitence, and when the sinful woman wept bitterly, the loving and holy Lord did not send her away without first forgiving her sins. You ought to remember the words of the thief hanging on the cross who turned to the Lord with all his heart and in the voice of one confessing said: "Remember me, Lord, when you come into your kingdom," and merited to hear immediately: "Today you shall be with me in paradise." My child, strengthened by these and many clear testimonies, come into the presence of the terrible judgments of God, who repays each one according to their works, and confess the sins which you have done at the instigation of the devil.   *Ordo Romano*

In confession the breakthrough to community takes place. Sin demands to have a person alone. It withdraws her from the community. The more isolated a person is, the more destructive will be the power of sin over her, and the more deeply she becomes involved in it, the more disastrous is her isolation. Sin wants to remain unknown. It shuns the light. In the darkness of the unexpressed it poisons the whole being of a person. This can happen even in the midst of a pious community.   Dietrich Bonhoeffer

MY father was a lonely man, but there's an awful lot of lonely men around. They won't say so, of course. Who tells the truth? You meet an old friend on the street. He looks like hell. It's frightening. His face is gray, and his hair's all falling out, and he's got the shakes. So you say, "Charlie, Charlie, you're looking *great*." So then he says, shaking all over, "I never felt better in my life, *never*." So then you go your way, and he goes his way.

John Cheever

MÁRGARÉT, áre you gríeving
Over Goldengrove unleaving?
Leáves, líke the things of man, you
With your fresh thoughts care for, can you?
Áh! ás the heart grows older
It will come to such sights colder
By and by, nor spare a sigh
Though worlds of wanwood leafmeal lie;
And yet you *will* weep and know why,
Now no matter, child, the name:
Sórrow's spríngs áre the same.
Nor mouth had, no nor mind, expressed
What heart heard of, ghost guessed:
It ís the blight man was born for,
It is Margaret you mourn for.

Gerard Manley
Hopkins
Nineteenth century

SUFFERING is the human struggle with and against pain. It is the experience of the breakdown of our systems of meaning and our stories about ourselves, and the struggle to restore those senses of safety and selfhood. Suffering in itself is neither noble nor redeeming. It is essentially an erosion of meaning. It is an interruption and destruction of those fundamental senses of safety and selfhood without which we cannot survive as individuals and as societies. Suffering only becomes redemptive or ennobling when we struggle against these corroding powers and rebuild ourselves in spite of the pain we are experiencing.   Robert J. Schreiter

THEY tell how it was, and how time
    came along, and how it happened
again and again. They tell
the slant life takes when it turns
and slashes your face as a friend.

Any wound is real. In church
a woman lets the sun find
her cheek, and we see the lesson:
there are years in that book; there are sorrows
a choir can't reach when they sing.

Rows of children lift their faces of promise,
places where the scars will be.   William Stafford

WHEN I first called Alienation to arrange an interview, he said he couldn't do it right now. "Everything is poisoned. Our speech is the language of captives. All attempts to communicate are futile or pretentious."

At that point I called around to find out more about his life story. It seems that he was a delightful child, curious and playful, and gentle. He was popular in art school and began his career sculpting massive figures. Although his work was praised, he could not reach the people he honored. Their indifference chilled him. He was hungry and frustrated, and his work became brutal and inaccessible. After his daughter was born, he gave up his studio and took a job downtown to support his family. He is very good at what he does, but it means nothing.

Alienation's associates are worried that he is really going crazy now. They miss the accuracy and insight of his sarcastic comments. As usual, he could say, "No one understands me." This time he doesn't care. He needs to be left alone. He is tearing off his masks. He is exploring the layers underneath the language of lies. He is in a labyrinth, and he is searching for Compassion. Though he hasn't found her yet, he sees the signs of her presence. He is recovering the pieces of his childhood self.

If you have an opportunity to talk to Alienation, don't lie to him or attempt to justify your compromises. Listen carefully. He is honest with himself. He will penetrate your mask.

J-Ruth Gendler

BEING human is an accomplishment like playing an instrument. It takes practice. The keys must be mastered. The old scores must be committed to memory. It is a skill we can forget. A little noise can make us forget the notes. The best of us is historical; the best of us is fragile. Being human is a second nature which history taught us, and which terror and deprivation can batter us into forgetting.

Michael Ignatieff

ONE thing i dont need
is any more apologies
i got sorry greetin me at my front door
you can keep yrs
i dont know what to do wit em
they dont open doors
or bring the sun back
they dont make me happy
or get a mornin paper
didnt nobody stop usin my tears to wash cars
cuz a sorry

i am simply tired
of collectin
   'i didnt know
    i was so important to you'
i'm gonna haveta throw some away
i cant get to the clothes in my closet
for alla the sorries
i'm gonna tack a sign to my door

leave a message by the phone
   'if you called
    to say yr sorry
    call somebody
    else
    i dont use em anymore'
i let sorry/didnt meanta/& how cd i know abt that
take a walk down a dark & musty street in brooklyn
i'm gonna do exactly what i want to
& i wont be sorry for none of it
letta sorry soothe yr soul/i'm gonna soothe mine

you were always inconsistent
doin somethin & then bein sorry
beatin my heart to death
talkin bout you sorry

Ntozake Shange

WE make ourselves a place apart
    Behind light words that tease and flout,
But oh, the agitated heart
    Till someone really finds us out.
'Tis pity if the case require
    (Or so we say) that in the end
We speak the literal to inspire
    The understanding of a friend.
But so with all, from babes that play
    At hide-and-seek to God afar,
So all who hide too well away
    Must speak and tell us where they are.

Robert Frost

THE outcast lepers would like to drag everything down in their ruin. And they become all the more evil, the more you cast them out; and the more you depict them as a court of lemures who want your ruin, the more they will be outcast. Saint Francis realized this, and his first decision was to go and live among the lepers. The people of God cannot be changed until the outcasts are restored to its body.

Umberto Eco

THEN my family fell apart, broke down, wailed like damaged angels as the wind bore down hard against our house and the radio played on without the slightest trace of pity. We wept hard with the gore of our attackers on our hands and faces, on our walls and furniture and floors. The statue of the infant Jesus lay beside me, covered with blood. In less than a minute he had killed the three men who had brought ruin and havoc to our home, and had established their incumbency in the heedless ordinance of nightmare. In our sleep they would rise from the dust of our terror and rape us a thousand times again. In immortal grandeur they would reassemble their torn bodies and burst into our rooms like evil khans, marauders, and conquerors, and we, again, would smell their breath in ours and feel our clothes ripped away from our bodies. Rape is a crime against sleep and memory; its afterimage imprints itself like an irreversible negative from the camera obscura of dreams. Throughout our lives these three dead and slaughtered men would teach us over and over of the abidingness, the terrible constancy, that accompanies a wound to the spirit. Though our bodies would heal, our souls had sustained a damage beyond compensation. Violence sends deep roots into the heart; it has no seasons; it is always ripe, evergreen.   Pat Conroy

MOTHER of God, Light in all darkness,
shelter Christ; our flame of hope, with your tender
    hands.
And in our times of dread and nightmares,
let him be our dream of comfort.
And in our times of physical pain and suffering,
let him be our healer.
And in our times of separation from God and one
another,
let him be our communion.

William Hart
McNichols

THE legend is whispered
in the women's tent
how the moon when she rises
full
follows some men into themselves
and changes them there
the season is short
but dreadful   shapeshifters
they wear strange hands
they walk through the houses
at night   their daughters
do not know them

who is there to protect her
from the hands of the father
not the windows which see and
say nothing   not the moon
that awful eye   not the woman
she will become with her
scarred tongue   who   who   who   the owl
laments into the evening   who
will protect her   this   prettylittlegirl

if the little girl lies
still enough
shut enough
hard enough
shapeshifter may not
walk tonight
the full moon may not
find him here
the hair on him
bristling
rising
up

the poem at the end of the world
is the poem the little girl breathes
into her pillow   the one
she cannot tell   the one
there is no one to hear   this poem
is a political poem   is a war poem   is a
universal poem but is not about
these things   this poem
is about one human heart   this poem
is the poem at the end of the world

Lucille Clifton

L ORD, will you ever remember me,
why keep turning away from me?
Must I carry this grief for ever,
how long endure this pain?
Psalm 13:2-3   Must my enemies always win?

F ORGIVENESS is the answer to the child's dream of a miracle by which what is broken is made whole again, what is soiled is again made clean. The dream explains why we need to be forgiven, and why we must forgive. In the presence of God, nothing stands between God and us — we *are* forgiven. But we *cannot* feel God's presence if anything is allowed to stand between ourselves and others.

Dag Hammarskjöld

T HIS is something we should never forget. That sick person, that alcoholic, that thief, are my brothers and sisters. It is possible that they find themselves abandoned in the street because no one gave them love and understanding. You and I could be in their place if we had not received love and understanding from other human beings.

Mother Teresa

T HE sense of being lost, displaced and homeless is pervasive in contemporary culture. The yearning to belong somewhere, to have a home, to be in a safe place is a deep and moving pursuit.

Walter Brueggemann

THE church must be ever ready to wash the disciples'
feet, a serving church, not a triumphalistic church,
biased in favor of the powerless to be their voice, to be in
solidarity with the poor and oppressed, the marginalized
ones — yes, preaching the gospel of reconciliation but
working for justice first, since there can never be real reconciliation without justice. It will demonstrate in its very
life that Jesus has broken down the wall of partition, and so
in its common life there will be no artificial barriers to any
Christian being able to participate fully.

Desmond Tutu

SAID General Oglethorpe to Wesley, "I never forgive."
"Then I hope, sir," said Wesley, "you never sin."

We hand folks over to God's mercy and show none ourselves.

George Eliot
Nineteenth century

NO one who is in love with himself is capable of loving
God.

Diadochus of Photice
Fifth century

B<small>UT WHEN HE CAME TO HIMSELF HE SAID,</small> "H<small>OW MANY OF MY</small>
<small>FATHER'S HIRED HANDS HAVE BREAD ENOUGH AND TO SPARE,</small>
<small>BUT HERE</small> I <small>AM DYING OF HUNGER!</small>"   Luke 15:17

~

Charles Dickens
Nineteenth century

M<small>AY</small> I tell you why it seems to me a good thing for us
to remember wrong that has been done us? That we
may forgive it.

Edward Hays

O Infinite Sea of Mercy,
make this unworthy servant
the channel of your gift of pardon,
that I also may be healed
as your forgiveness passes through me to others.

Dag Hammarskjöld

W<small>E</small> cannot afford to forget any experience, not even
the most painful.

THE spirit of Almighty God made all things and searches out hidden things in hidden places. Surely God knows your imaginations and what you think in your hearts! Woe to those who sin and want to hide their sins! Because the Lord will strictly examine all their works, and will make a public spectacle of all of you. And when your sins come out before others, you shall be put to shame; and your own iniquities shall stand as your accusers in that day. What will you do? Or how will you hide your sins before God and the angels? Behold, God is the judge, tremble! Cease from your sins, and forget your iniquities, never to commit them again; so God will lead you forth and deliver you from all tribulations.   Ezra 4:62–67

BY the tender mercy of our God,
     the dawn from on high will break upon us,
to give light to those who sit in darkness
          and in the shadow of death,
     to guide our feet into the way of peace.   Luke 1:78–79

WE are reminded in many ways of the quiet ministry of the spirit of the living God in our lives and in life that abounds around us. The little healings of the silent breaches, the great redemptive acts when times are out of joint, the lifting of our horizons of hope when to have hope seems to be against all wisdom and against all judgment, the stirring of the will to forgive when for so long a time we have been buried under an avalanche of great hostilities — there are so many ways by which the ministry of the living God tutors the spirit, corrects the times, gives lift to the days.   Howard Thurman

M Y own heart let me more have pity on; let
Me live to my sad self hereafter kind,
Charitable; not live this tormented mind
With the tormented mind tormenting yet.

I cast for comfort I can no more get
By groping around my comfortless, than blind
Eyes in their dark can day or thirst can find
Thirst's all-in-all in all a world of wet.

Soul, self; come, poor Jackself, I do advise
You, jaded, let be; call off thoughts awhile
Elsewhere; leave comfort root-room; let joy size

At God knows when to God knows what; whose smile
's not wrung, see you; unforeseen times rather — as skies
Betweenpie mountains — lights a lovely mile.

Gerard Manley
Hopkins
Nineteenth century

T HERE can be no future at all for us unless we are able to
speak of forgiveness. If there is no forgiveness, we
remain locked in the past, prisoners of previous mistakes
and misunderstandings, unable ever to begin again. Apart
from forgiveness, all hope of creativity is gone; the risks
involved in creativeness are beyond imagining without the
assurance that it is possible to find reconciliation on the far
side of our failures, betrayals and all the hurts that we inflict.
Without forgiveness there can be no enduring community
of any sort. Without it, everything remains as fractured as
ever, and the conflicts must still rage among those who, like
ourselves, are enemies and strangers, sinners and ungodly.
But forgiveness cannot be embraced without a deepened
awareness of the importance of order and of the guilt
incurred by its violation.

David Baily Harned

I N confession the light of the gospel breaks into the darkness and seclusion of the heart. The sin must be brought
into the light. The unexpressed must be openly spoken and
acknowledged. All that is secret and hidden is made manifest. It is a hard struggle until the sin is openly admitted. But
God breaks gates of brass and bars of iron (Psalm 107:16).   Deitrich Bonhoeffer

F OR a scientist, this is a good way to live and die, maybe
the ideal way for any of us — excitedly finding we were
wrong and excitedly waiting for tomorrow to come so we
can start over, get our new dope together, and find a
Hypothesis Number One all over again. And being basi-
cally on the right track when we are wrong.   Norman Maclean

O LD paint on canvas, as it ages, sometimes becomes
transparent. When that happens it is possible, in some
pictures, to see the original lines: a tree will show through
a woman's dress, a child makes way for a dog, a large boat
is no longer on an open sea. That is called *pentimento*
because the painter "repented," changed his mind. Perhaps
it would be as well to say that the old conception, replaced
by a later choice, is a way of seeing and then seeing again.   Lillian Hellman

Romans 8:26–27

L IKEWISE the Spirit helps us in our weakness; for we do not know how to pray as we ought, but that very Spirit intercedes with sighs too deep for words. And God, who searches the heart, knows what is the mind of the Spirit, because the Spirit intercedes for the saints according to the will of God.

Augustine of Hippo
Fifth century

L ATE have I loved you, O Beauty ever ancient, ever new, late have I loved you! You were within me, but I was outside, and it was there that I searched for you. In my unloveliness I plunged into the lovely things which you created. You were with me but I was not with you. Created things kept me from you; yet if they had not been in you they would not have been at all. You called, you shouted, and you broke through my deafness. You flashed, you shone, and you dispelled my blindness. You breathed your fragrance on me; I drew in breath and now I pant for you. I have tasted you, now I hunger and thirst for more. You touched me, and I burned for your peace.

Never shall I forget that night, the first night in camp, which has turned my life into one long night, seven times cursed and seven times sealed. Never shall I forget that smoke. Never shall I forget the little faces of the children, whose bodies I saw turned into wreaths of smoke beneath a silent blue sky.

Never shall I forget those flames which consumed my faith forever.

Never shall I forget that nocturnal silence which deprived me, for all eternity, of the desire to live. Never shall I forget those moments which murdered my God and my soul and turned my dreams to dust. Never shall I forget these things even if I am condemned to live as long as God. Never.   Elie Wiesel

I am running into a new year
and the old years blow back
like a wind
that i catch in my hair
like strong fingers like
all my old promises and
it will be hard to let go
of what i said to myself
about myself
when i was sixteen and
twentysix and thirtysix
even thirtysix but
i am running into a new year
and i beg what i love
and i leave to forgive me   Lucille Clifton

WE have sinned against life by failing to work for peace.

We have sinned against life by keeping silent in the face of injustice.

We have sinned against life by ignoring those who suffer in distant lands.

We have sinned against life by forgetting the poor in our own midst.

We have failed to respect those made in the image of God.

We have withheld our love from those who depend on us.

We have engaged in gossip and in repeated slander.

We have distorted the truth for our own advantage.

We have conformed to fashion and not to conscience.

We have indulged in despair and trafficked with cynics.

We have given meager support to our Houses of Study.

We have neglected our heritage of learning.

We have sinned against ourselves and paid scant heed to the life of the spirit.

We have sinned against ourselves and have not risen to fulfill the best that is in us.

Preparatory service for the Days of Awe

For all these, O God of mercy, forgive us, pardon us, grant us atonement!

Exterior penances are done chiefly for three ends:

First, as satisfaction for the sins committed;

Second, to conquer oneself — that is, to make sensuality obey reason and all inferior parts be more subject to the superior;

Third, to seek and find some grace or gift which the person wants and desires; as, for instance, if he desires to have interior contrition for his sins, or to weep much over them, or over the pains and sufferings which Christ our Lord suffered in His Passion, or to settle some doubt in which the person finds himself.

Ignatius of Loyola

The abbot Macarius said, "If we dwell upon the harms that have been wrought on us by humankind, we amputate from our mind the power of dwelling upon God."

Sayings of the Desert Fathers

Let the abbot exercise all diligence in his care for erring brothers, for they that are in health need not a physician, but they that are sick (Matthew 9:12). He ought, therefore, as a wise physician, to use every remedy in his power. Let him send *senpectae,* that is old and prudent brothers, who may, as it were, secretly comfort the troubled brother, inducing him to make humble satisfaction and consoling him lest he be swallowed up with overmuch sorrow (2 Corinthians 2:7).

The Rule of Benedict

WHILE we are still on earth, let us repent. For we are as clay in the hand of a potter. Just as the potter, if he misshapes or breaks a vessel in his hands while he is making it, shapes it over again if he has not already put it into the fiery oven, when he can do nothing more; let us as well, while we are still in the world and have the time to repent of the evil we have committed with our flesh, let us do so with our whole heart, that the Lord will save us while there is time for repentance.

Clement of Rome
Second century

YEARS and miles ago in a high country
one morning the sun shone into a cave — splendid
paints leaped into color. A mysterious artist
had worked by candlelight on the walls in secret.

Rockslides now have hidden that room. No chart
or path or tunnel penetrates, no person remembers.
All of history has turned aside from that glimpse
the sun had; nobody believes in that room anymore.

William Stafford   It is there.

To trivialize and ignore memory is to trivialize and ignore human identity, and to trivialize and ignore human identity is to trivialize and ignore human dignity.

Robert J. Schreiter

PEOPLE who have a religion should be glad, for not everyone has the gift of believing in heavenly things. You don't necessarily even have to be afraid of punishment after death; purgatory, hell and heaven are things that a lot of people can't accept, but still a religion, it doesn't matter which, keeps a person on the right path. It isn't the fear of God but the upholding of one's own honor and conscience. How noble and good everyone could be if, every evening before falling asleep, they were to recall to their minds the events of the whole day and consider exactly what has been good and bad. Then, without realizing it, you try to improve yourself at the start of each new day; of course, you achieve quite a lot in the course of time. Anyone can do this, it costs nothing and is certainly very helpful. Whoever doesn't know it must learn and find by experience that: "A quiet conscience makes one strong!"

Anne Frank

THAT's why we love disaster, Harry sees, it puts us back in touch with guilt and sends us crawling back to God. Without a sense of being in the wrong we're no better than animals.

John Updike

CONSCIENCE: the inner voice which warns us that some-one may be looking.

H. L. Mencken

EACH of us enters our own wilderness once in a while; infrequently, if we are lucky, but at least once, and maybe more often, and maybe also for a long time. Deserts seem then to stretch endlessly ahead; oases dissipate into mirages. Our stamina flags. But the story of our ancestors reminds us that we can get through. The Promised Land of milk and honey lies somewhere in the distance. And in the meantime we number the things within us that God has supplied for just such times as this, the day-by-day miracles that sustain us, and for which we give thanks.

Lawrence A. Hoffman

I cannot and will not cut my conscience to fit this year's fashions.

Lillian Hellman

REMORSE is memory awake,
Her parties all astir,
A presence of departed acts
At window and at door.

It's past set down before the soul
And lighted with a match,
Perusal to facilitate
And help belief to stretch.

Remorse is cureless — the disease
Not even God can heal,
For 'tis his institution and
The adequate of hell.

Emily Dickinson
Nineteenth century

I remember the ancient days,
I recall your wonders,
the work of your hands.
Dry as thirsty land,
I reach out for you.

Answer me quickly, Lord.
My strength is spent.
Do not hide from me
or I will fall into the grave.

Let morning announce your love,
for it is you I trust.
Show me the right way,
I offer you myself.

Rescue me from my foes,
you are my only refuge, Lord.
Teach me your will,
for you are my God.

Graciously lead me, Lord,
on to level ground.
I call on your just name,
keep me safe, free from danger.

In your great love for me,
disarm my enemies,
destroy their power,
for I belong to you.   Psalm 143:5 – 12

A certain tribe in Africa traps wild monkeys in a very ingenious way. They take a gourd or pumpkin and hollow out the inside and then they cut a hole just big enough for a monkey's hand to squeeze through. Then they throw peanuts inside the pumpkin, tie it to a tree and leave. When all is quiet, the monkeys investigate, smell the bait, reach in to get the peanuts, make a fist and then try to squeeze out the same way. But the opening is too small for the fist to get out and the only way they can hang on to the peanuts is by making a fist. So they stuck. The next day, they scream with rage and fear as the natives pick them up and ship them off to live in some zoo forever.

Anonymous

WHAT is there in my heart that you should sue
so fiercely for its love? What kind of care
brings you as though a stranger to my door
through the long night and the icy dew

seeking the heart that will harbor you,
that keeps itself religiously secure?
At this dark solstice filled with frost and fire
your passion's ancient wounds must bleed anew.

So many nights the angel of my house
has fed such urgent comfort through a dream,
whispered 'your lord is coming, he is close'

that I have drowsed half-faithful for a time
bathed in pure tones of promise and remorse:
Geoffrey Hill   'tomorrow I shall wake to welcome him.'

ONCE a brother in Scete was found guilty, and the older bothers came in assembly and sent to the abbot Moses, asking him to come: but he would not. Then the priest sent to him, saying: "Come, for the assembly of brothers awaits." And he rose up and came. But taking with him a very old basket, he filled it with sand and carried it behind him. And they went out to meet him, asking, "Father, what is this?" And the old man said to them, "My sins are running behind me and I do not see them, and I am come today to judge the sins of another." And they heard him, and said naught to the brother, but forgave him.

*Sayings of the
Desert Fathers*

WHAT is needed here is not a small act of love. It is something fundamental and important and difficult. To love your parents deep inside. To forgive them for all the trouble they have given you by their very existence: by tying you down, by adding the burden of their own complicated lives to your own.

Etty Hillesum

HE will turn the hearts of parents to their children and the hearts of the children to their parents, so that I will not come and strike the land with a curse.

Malachi 4:6

BEHOLD I am bending the knees of my heart before you; and I am beseeching your kindness.
I have sinned, O Lord, I have sinned;
and I certainly know my sins.

Prayer of Manasseh

I beseech you: forgive me, O Lord, forgive me!

GOD in Heaven, you have helped my life to grow like a tree. Now something has happened. Satan, like a bird, has carried in one twig of his own choosing after another. Before I knew it he had built a dwelling place and was living in it. Tonight, my Father, I am throwing out both the bird and the nest.

Nigerian prayer

HOW will people be convinced that we believe what we preach if they see that we are too cowardly to denounce injustices in the spirit of the gospel out of fear of reprisals on our person or our work?

Pedro Arrupe

John Henry Newman
Nineteenth century

IN the higher world it is otherwise, but here below to live is to change and to be perfect is to have changed often.

A ʟʟ of ministry rests on the conviction that nothing, absolutely nothing, in our lives is outside the realm of God's judgment and mercy. By hiding parts of our story, not only from our own consciousness but also from God's eye, we claim a divine role for ourselves; we become judges of our own past and limit mercy to our own fears. Thus we disconnect ourselves not only from our own suffering but also from God's suffering for us. The challenge of ministry is to help people in very concrete situations — people with illnesses or in grief, people with physical or mental handicaps, people suffering from poverty and oppression, people caught in the complex networks of secular or religious institutions — to see and experience their story as part of God's ongoing redemptive work in the world. These insights and experiences heal precisely because they restore the broken connection between the world and God and create a new unity in which memories that formerly seemed only destructive are now reclaimed as part of a redemptive event.

Henri J. M. Nouwen

A ᴍᴏɴɢ the harp-like morning-glory strings,
Taut with the dew from garden bed to eaves,
As if she played unheard some tenderness
That wrought on him beside her in the night.
"Warren," she said, "he has come home to die:
You needn't be afraid he'll leave you this time."

"Home," he mocked gently.

"Yes, what else but home?
It all depends on what you mean by home.
Of course he's nothing to us, any more
Than was the hound that came a stranger to us
Out of the woods, worn out upon the trail."

"Home is the place where, when you have to go there,
They have to take you in."

Robert Frost

I WILL GET UP AND GO TO MY FATHER, AND I WILL SAY TO HIM,
"FATHER, I HAVE SINNED AGAINST HEAVEN AND BEFORE YOU; I
AM NO LONGER WORTHY TO BE CALLED YOUR SON; TREAT ME
LIKE ONE OF YOUR HIRED HANDS." Luke 15:18–19

~

A sinner who wanted to atone came to the rabbi of Roptchitz to learn what penance he should do. He was ashamed to confess all his sins to the zaddik and yet he had to disclose each and every one, for otherwise the rabbi could not have told him the proper form of atonement. So he said that one of his friends had done such and such a thing, but had been too ashamed to come in person and had commissioned him to go in his stead and find out for him the purification for every one of his sins.

Rabbi Naftali looked smilingly into the man's sly and tense face. "Your friend," he said, "is a fool. He could easily have come to me himself and pretended to represent someone who was ashamed to come in his own person."

Unknown

CONFESS your sins to one another, and pray for one another, so that you may be healed. The prayer of the righteous is powerful and effective.

James 5:16

MY God,
I am sorry for my sins with all my heart.
In choosing to do wrong
and failing to do good,
I have sinned against you
whom I should love above all things.
I firmly intend, with your help,
to do penance,
to sin no more,
and to avoid whatever leads me to sin.
Our Savior Jesus Christ
suffered and died for us.
In his name, my God, have mercy.   Rite of penance

THEN Peter came and said to him, "Lord, if another member of the church sins against me, how often should I forgive? As many as seven times?" Jesus said to him, "Not seven times, but, I tell you, seventy-seven times."   Matthew 18:21 – 22

FORGIVE us, our Father, for all the things of which we are so poignantly aware and for those failures of will that have made it so difficult for us to respond to your will. Walk with us in the long, perilous journey which stretches out before us and give to our faltering footsteps the great, strong rhythm of the purposes of God.   Howard Thurman

I shall now leave you breathless with the strange and won-drous tale of this sturdy lad's adventures today in down-town Oz. Picture, if you will, me. I am walking on East Fifty-first Street an hour ago, and I decided to construct and develop a really decorative, general-all-purpose apology. Not complicated, just the words "I am sorry," and with a lit-tle style. (Sorry for what? you ask.) Anything. For being late, early, stupid, asleep, silly, alive. Well, y'know when you're walking down the street talking to yourself how sometimes you suddenly say a coupla words out loud? So I said, "I'm sorry," and this fella, complete stranger, he looks up a sec-ond and says, "That's all right, Mac," and goes right on.

He automatically forgave me. I communicated. Five-o'clock rush-hour in midtown you could say, "Sir, I believe your hair is on fire," and they wouldn't hear you. So I decided to test the whole thing out scientifically, I stayed right down there on the corner of Fifty-first and Lex for a while, just saying, "I'm sorry" to everybody that went by.

(Abjectly) "Oh, I'm sorry, sir . . ."

(Slowly, quaveringly) "I'm terribly sorry, madam . . ."

(Warmly) "Say there, miss, I'm sorry."

Of course, some people just gave me a funny look, but I swear, seventy-five percent of them *forgave* me.

"Forget it, buddy . . ."

"That's OK, really."

Two ladies forgave me in unison, one fella forgave me from a passing car, one guy forgave me for his dog. "Poofer forgives the nice man, don't you, Poofer?"

It was fabulous. I had tapped some vast reservoir. Something had happened to all of them for which they felt *some*body should apologize. If you went up to people on the street and offered them money, they'd refuse it. But everybody accepts apology immediately. It is the most negotiable currency. I said to them, "I'm sorry." And they were all so generous, so kind. You could give 'em love and it wouldn't be accepted as graciously, as unquestioningly.

I could run up on the roof right now and holler, "I am sorry," and half a million people would holler right back, "That's OK, just see that you don't do it again!"

Herb Gardner

CHRIST will come to your grave, and if he finds there weeping for you Martha, the woman of good service, and Mary, who carefully heard the word of God, like holy church which has chosen the best part, he will be moved with compassion, when at your death he shall see the tears of many and will say: "Where have you laid him?" that is to say, in what condition of guilt is he? in which rank of penitents? I would see him for whom ye weep, that he himself may move me with his tears. I will see if he is already dead to that sin for which forgiveness is entreated.

Ambrose of Milan
Fourth century

IN a certain month of winter, one dark and cloudy night followed upon the other; the moon was hidden and Rabbi Barukh could not say the blessing of the moon. On the last night of those set aside for this, he sent someone out to look at the sky, time after time, but again and again he was told that it was dark as pitch and the snow was falling thick and fast. Finally he said: "If things were with me as they should be, the moon would surely do me a favor! So I ought to do penance. But because I am no longer strong enough to do it, I must at least penitently confess my sins." And this penitent confession broke from his lips with such force that all who were there with him were shaken. A great shudder pulsed through their hearts, and they turned to God. Then someone came and reported: "It isn't snowing anymore. You can see a little light!" The rabbi put on his coat and went out. The clouds were scattered. Among the shining stars shone the moon, and he spoke the blessing.

Martin Buber

OUR God and God of our ancestors, let our prayer reach you — do not turn away from our pleading. For we are not so arrogant and obstinate to claim that we are indeed righteous people and have never sinned. But we know that both we and our ancestors have sinned.

We have abused and betrayed. We are cruel.

We have destroyed and embittered other people's lives.

We were false to ourselves.

We have gossiped about others and hated them.

We have insulted and jeered. We have killed. We have lied.

We have misled others and neglected them.

We were obstinate. We have perverted and quarrelled.

We have robbed and stolen.

We have transgressed through unkindness.

We have been both violent and weak.

We have practiced extortion.

We have yielded to wrong desires, our zeal was misplaced.

We turn away from your commandments and good judgment but it does not help us. Your justice exists whatever happens to us, for you work for truth, but we bring about evil. What can we say before you — so distant is the place where you are found? And what can we tell you — your being is remote as the heavens? Yet you know everything, hidden and revealed. You know the mysteries of the universe and the intimate secrets of everyone alive. You probe our body's state. You see into the heart and mind. Nothing escapes you, nothing is hidden from your gaze. Our God and God of our ancestors, have mercy on us and pardon all our sins; grant atonement for all our iniquities, forgiveness for all our transgressions.

Prayer for the
Day of Atonement

COME, let us return to the LORD;
    for it is he who has torn, and he will heal us;
he has struck down, and he will bind us up.
After two days he will revive us;
    on the third day he will raise us up,
    that we may live before him.
Let us know, let us press on to know the LORD;
    his appearing is as sure as the dawn;
he will come to us like the showers,
    like the spring rains that water the earth.
What shall I do with you, O Ephraim?
    What shall I do with you, O Judah?
Your love is like a morning cloud,
    like the dew that goes away early.
Therefore I have hewn them by the prophets,
    I have killed them by the words of my mouth,
    and my judgment goes forth as the light.
For I desire steadfast love and not sacrifice.

Hosea 6:1–6   the knowledge of God rather than burnt offerings.

FORGIVE me, most gracious Lord, if this day I have done
or said anything to increase the pain of the world.

F. B. Meyer

I detected in her voice another quality which I find admirable—the quality of desperation. Desperation and truth are closely akin—the desperate confession can usually be trusted, and just as it is not given to everyone to make a deathbed confession, so the capacity for desperation is granted to very few, and I was not one of them.   Graham Greene

FATHER of mercy,
like the prodigal son
I return to you and say:
"I have sinned against you
and am no longer worthy to be called your son."
Christ Jesus, Savior of the world,
I pray with the repentant thief
to whom you promised paradise:
"Lord, remember me in your kingdom."
Holy Spirit, fountain of love,
I call on you with trust:
"Purify my heart,
and help me to walk as a child of the light."   Rite of penance

Pity me, Lord,
I hurt all over;
my eyes are swollen,
my heart and body ache.

Grief consumes my life,
sighs fill my days;
guilt saps my strength,
my bones dissolve.

Enemies mock me,
make me the butt of jokes.
Neighbors scorn me,
strangers avoid me.
Forgotten like the dead,
I am a shattered jar.

I hear the crowd whisper,
"Attack on every side!"
as they scheme to take my life.

But I trust in you, Lord.
I say, "You are my God,
my life is in your hands."
Snatch me from the enemy,
ruthless in their chase.

Look on me with love,
save your servant.
I call on you;
save me from shame!

Psalm 31:10–18a

L ET us review all the generations in turn, and learn that from generation to generation the Master has given an opportunity for repentance to those who desire to turn to him. Noah preached repentance, and those who obeyed were saved. Jonah preached destruction to the people of Nineveh; but they, repenting of their sins, made atonement to God by their prayers and received salvation, even though they were alienated from God.

The ministers of the grace of God spoke about repentance through the Holy Spirit; indeed, the Master of the universe himself spoke about the repentance with an oath: "For as I live, says the Lord, I do not desire the death of the sinner, so much as repentance."

Clement of Rome
Second century

A ND pray to God to have mercy upon us
And I pray that I may forget
These matters that with myself I too much discuss
Too much explain
Because I do not hope to turn again
Let these words answer
For what is done, not to be done again
May the judgment not be too heavy upon us.

Because these wings are no longer wings to fly
But merely vans to beat the air
The air which is now thoroughly small and dry
Smaller and dryer than the will
Teach us to care and not to care
Teach us to sit still.

Pray for us sinners now and at the hour of our death
Pray for us now and at the hour of our death.

T. S. Eliot

IN these dark days when negation has so deeply entered
    into thought,
and the futility of life oppresses many souls,
when belief and unbelief appear indifferent
and what is left
    is natural passion to express the pride of life,
    or the empty void of nothingness
    when the nerve to live and to create is weakened
    and suicides increase —
O Lord, forgive the failures of your church to witness
    to the world
    that justice should run down as water
    and righteousness a mighty stream,
O Lord, forgive the failure of the Christian life
    that lives so worldly
    that few can see the life of Spirit
    that must proclaim the kingdom of God's love
Gilbert Shaw   to glorify his Name.

WE all have committed offenses; together we confess these human sins:

The sins of arrogance, bigotry, and cynicism; of deceit and egotism, flattery and greed, injustice and jealousy.

Some of us kept grudges, were lustful, malicious or narrow-minded.

Others were obstinate or possessive, quarrelsome, rancorous or selfish.

There was violence, weakness of will, xenophobia:

We yielded to temptation, and showed zeal for bad causes.

Now may it be Your will, O Lord God of all the generations, to pardon all our sins, to forgive all our wrongdoings, and to blot out all our transgressions.

Preparatory service for the Days of Awe

THERE are two wonderful lines in King Lear, "When thou dost ask me blessing, I'll kneel down and ask thee for forgiveness." If an old person does not feel the need to be forgiven by the young, he or she certainly has not grown into age, but merely fallen into it, and his or her "blessing" would be worth nothing. The lines convey with the utmost brevity and power the truth that the blessing that the old may pass on to the young springs only out of that humility that is the fruit of wholeness, the humility that knows *how* to kneel, *how* to ask forgiveness. The old man kneels, not in order to ease guilt feelings (which is at the root of so much apologizing) but in the full and free acceptance of that which Charles Williams called *co-inherence.* King Lear does not say, "I am not worthy to bless you, only to grovel at your feet." He says, "When you ask me blessing, I'll kneel. . . ." The kneeling is the blessing.

Helen M. Luke

Martin Luther
Sixteenth century

DEAR Lord God, I cannot count the sins that I have done and still do. I have forgotten most of them and no longer feel my guilt. All that is in me and all power that is not grace is sin and is condemned. My works and my powers only make me despondent. I do not know what else to do but to hope and pray for your mercy. As grace and faith control me, I am devout through Christ. Where these fail me, I know and confess that nothing good is left in me. No matter how long I live, it will never be different. If I had the holiness of all monks, there would still be nothing good in what I think, speak, live, and do, if it did not have your divine grace and power. All my sins are forgiven out of pure grace. This is the joy and comfort which you gladly grant to me, a poor sinner. Amen.

Clement of Rome
Second century

LET us repent immediately. Let us be clear-headed regarding the good, for we are full of much stupidity and wickedness. Let us wipe off from ourselves our former sins and be saved, repenting from the very souls of our being. And let us not seek to please others. But let us not desire to please only ourselves with our righteousness, but also those who are outsiders, that the Name may not be blasphemed on our account.

I confess to almighty God,
and to you, my brothers and sisters,
that I have sinned through my own fault
in my thoughts and in my words,
in what I have done,
and in what I have failed to do;
and I ask blessed Mary ever virgin,
all the angels and saints,
and you, my brothers and sisters,
to pray for me to the Lord our God.   Roman rite

ETERNAL God, what can we say in your presence? How
account for our sins? We speak of repentance, and yet
are slow to change. But now we turn to you with the prayer
that your love may abide with us always, turning our hearts
to your ways, our feet to your paths. Hope is food and drink
to us; hope sustains us. And so we pray: Do not turn us
away empty-handed from your presence. End our darkness
with your light and turn our passions to your purpose. Help
us, Lord, in this hour of turning, to make real in our lives   Preparatory service for
the words of our mouths, the meditations of our hearts.   the Days of Awe

Wᴵᴸᵀ thou forgive that sinn where I begunn,
  Which is my sinn, though it were done before?
Wilt thou forgive those sinns, through which I runn,
  And doe them still, though still I doe deplore?
    When thou hast done, thou hast not done,
      for I have more.

Wilt thou forgive that sinn, by which I have wonne
  Others to sinn, and made my sinn their dore?
Wilt thou forgive that sinn which I did shunne
  A yeare, or twoe, but wallowed in a score?
    When thou hast done, thou hast not done,
      for I have more.

I have a sinn of fear, that when I have spunn
  My last thred, I shall perish on the shore;
Sweare by thy selfe that at my death thy Sunn
  Shall shine as it shines nowe, and heretofore;
    And having done that, thou hast done,
      I have noe more.

John Donne
Seventeenth century

Aꜱꜱᴜʀᴇᴅʟʏ, the celebration of Lauds and Vespers must never pass by without the prioress or abbot reciting the entire Prayer of Jesus at the end for all to hear, because thorns of contention are likely to spring up. Thus warned by the pledge they make to one another in the very words of this prayer: "Forgive us as we forgive" (Matthew 6:12), they may cleanse themselves of this kind of vice. At other celebrations, only the final part of this prayer is said aloud, that all may reply: "But deliver us from evil" (Matthew 6:13).

The Rule of Benedict

THE act of confiding in human sympathy, the consciousness that a fellow-being was listening to her with patient
pity, prepared her soul for that stronger leap by which faith
grasps the idea of the divine sympathy.

George Eliot
Nineteenth century

ON Friday afternoon Milly stopped at Ernie's Cards 'n
Things to buy a *mea culpa* card for her father-in-law
whom she had apparently insulted.

"Sorry," Ernie's wife said in her testy way. "We're all out."

Milly found this hard to believe. The card rack was full. You
could buy a happiness-in-your-new-home card or a mind-
your-own-beeswax card, even a spectacular three-dollar
pop-up card announcing to the world that you were feeling
underappreciated. Surely there was such a thing as an I'm-
sorry card.

"You can believe what you want," Ernie's wife said. "But
we're sold right out. At the start of the week I had at least
a dozen sorry cards in stock. We have a real nice selection,
all the way from 'I boobed' to 'Forgive me, Dear Heart.'
They went like hotcakes, the whole lot. That's more than I
sell in an average year."

"How strange," Milly said. "What on earth's everyone being
sorry about all of a sudden?"

Carol Shields

PRIEST

Are you suffering from pride?

PENITENT

What is pride?

PRIEST

To be proud is to go above others: when, therefore, you extol yourself above all others, then you are proud.

PENITENT

I do this frequently and from habit.

PRIEST

Beg forgiveness and leave off this thing.

PENITENT

I am sorry, Father, and by the grace of God, I will leave off this thing.

Liber Penitentialis

Lord, you return gladly and lovingly to lift up the one who offends you and I do not turn to raise up and honor the one who angers me.

John of the Cross
Sixteenth century

Blessed are the merciful, for they will receive mercy.

Matthew 5:7

Now is the time for turning. The leaves are beginning to turn from green to red to orange. The birds are beginning to run and heading once more toward the South. The animals are beginning to turn to storing their food for the winter. For leaves, birds and animals turning comes instinctively. But for us turning does not come so easily. It takes an act of will for us to make a turn. It means breaking with old habits. It means admitting that we have been wrong; and this is never easy. It means losing face; it means starting all over again; and this is always painful. It means saying: I am sorry. It means recognizing that we have the ability to change. These things are terribly hard to do. But unless we turn, we will be trapped forever in yesterday's ways.

Preparatory service for the Days of Awe

When I look back upon my life nigh spent,
Nigh spent, although the stream as yet flows on,
I more of follies than of sins repent,
Less for offence than love's shortcomings moan.
With self, O Father, leave me not alone —
Leave not with the beguiler the beguiled;
Besmirched and ragged, Lord, take back thine own:
A fool I bring thee to be made a child.

George MacDonald
Nineteenth century

Lᴏʀᴅ, I give myself to you.

I trust you, God;
do not fail me,
nor let my enemies gloat.
No one loyal is shamed,
but traitors know disgrace.

Teach me how to live,
Lord, show me the way.
Steer me toward your truth,
you, my saving God,
you, my constant hope.

Recall your tenderness,
your lasting love.
Remember me, not my faults,
the sins of my youth.
To show your own goodness,
God, remember me.

Good and just is the Lord,
guiding those who stray.
God leads the poor,
pointing out the path.

God's ways are faithful love
for those who keep the covenant.
Be true to your name, O Lord,
Psalm 25:1–11   forgive my sin, though great.

WITH you I take refuge, Lord,
and to you I will shout, Lord,
to you I will pour out my supplication,
to you I will confess my sins,
and to you I will reveal my lawless deeds.
Spare me, Lord,
because I have sinned much before you,
I have committed lawlessness and irreverence,
and have said wicked and unspeakable things before you.
My mouth defiled from the sacrifices of the idols
and from the tables of the gods of the Egyptians.
I have sinned, Lord,
before you I have sinned much in ignorance,
and have worshiped dead and dumb idols.
And now I am not worthy to open my mouth to you, Lord.   Joseph and Aseneth

IT must be a simple, humble confession, plain, faithful,
And also frequent, revealing, discreet, liberating, modest,
Complete, secret, sorrowful, swift,
Courageous, and accusing, and it must prepare one to   Thomas Aquinas
    carry out one's promises.   Thirteenth century

Have mercy on us, Lord.
For we have sinned against you.

Show us your steadfast love, O God.

Roman rite   And grant us your salvation.

The new year ceremony of the northern Ashanti of Ghana is called *Apo*. The word derives from a root meaning "to speak roughly or harshly." Another name for the ceremony means "to wash" or "to cleanse." It is a time when grudges and hostilities can be openly expressed, especially against the king. For the Ashanti, like other peoples, believe that harbored grudges and pent-up resentments can eventually injure both those who hold them and the people against whom they are held. Since powerful officials are more likely to offend the common people, rather than the other way around, it is they who bear the brunt of the accusations during the Apo celebrations. In this way people free their hearts of dangerous feelings which might otherwise lead to witchcraft and to physical illness. According to an old Ashanti priest:

Our forbears knew this to be the case, and so they ordained a time, once every year, when every man and woman, free man and slave, should have the freedom to speak out just what was in their head, to tell their neighbors just what they thought of them, and of their actions, and not only to their neighbors, but also the king and chief. When a man has spoken freely thus, he will feel his *sunsum* [soul] cool and quieted, and the *sunsum* of the other person against whom he has now openly spoken will be quieted also. The King of the Ashanti may have killed your children, and you hate him. This has made him ill, and you ill, too; when you are allowed to say before his face what you think, you both benefit.

Benjamin C. Ray

Have mercy, Lord, have mercy.
We have swallowed enough scorn,
stomached enough sneers:
the scoffing of the complacent,
the mockery of the proud.

Psalm 123:3–4

To know full forgiveness and the first stirrings of a healing, we must yield our self-sufficiency. Forgiveness is essentially a surrender to those others, God as well as a faithful community, who alone can give us the healing we absolutely need but can never offer ourselves.

Paul J. Wadell

A man cannot forgive up to four hundred and ninety times without forgiveness becoming a part of the habit structure of his being. Forgiveness is not an occasional act; it is a permanent attitude.

Martin Luther King, Jr.

So he set off and went to his father.   Luke 15:20

~

The process of healing or being reconciled is also a coming of age, a taking of responsibility for our lives. Negative guilt and anxiety can often hold us in a prison which in a paradoxical way can be strangely congenial. As long as I am locked in this state I have the perfect alibi for not engaging with life. We need great trust in God working in us as we allow ourselves to live and discover the freedom that is the other side of all the brokenness that has hitherto cramped and even paralyzed our lives.

Wilfrid McGreal

Each footstep, Ian felt, led him closer to something important. He was acutely conscious all at once of motion, of flux and possibility. He felt he was an arrow—not an arrow shot by God but an arrow heading toward God, and if it took every bit of this only life he had, he believed that he would get there in the end.

Anne Tyler

SEVEN years ago
at forty five
i knew it was time
for a rock bottom change
time to kick over my traces
time to stand my life on its head
time to sow my autonomous oats
time to put my money where my mouth was

because i couldn't bear not to
                              any longer

which is not to say
it happened in one night
or even in one year
by magic and by spells
aided by rational and sympathetic talk
with my family
(quite the contrary)
that it was trauma free
that i didn't have
insomnia backache guilt anxiety frantic fears
savage rages homicidal scenes suicidal sobbings
that for a long time i didn't become
someone unrecognisable
to myself
but it was literally
                      change or die

because of being middle aged
not despite it
because of knowing in my gut
time was jogging onwards
and i deserved something
                better
                        for myself
                              now
or never   Astra

To enter into a process of reconciliation is better described as entering a *mysterion,* a pathway in which God leads us out of suffering and alienation into the experience of the grace of reconciliation. This grace is transforming, and creates the conditions of possibility not only for our forgiving our enemies, but also helping them rediscover their humanity.

Robert J. Schreiter

Sin in human life is manifested in the inability to escape alienation in denial of the victory of Christ over sin. The church, correspondingly, is the privileged place where alienation is overcome by experiencing the victory of Christ in community. . . . When someone validly and authentically assumes a place at the table, that person is fully incorporated into the community. It is a matter of engaging the heart and the mind, of inspiring action and conviction. To gather validly and authentically at the community's table means an acceptance of the life of the community. That acceptance is not merely a passive consent; it is an active involvement in the common life of apostles and witnesses who recognize the risen Lord in the breaking of the bread. It is an acceptance of the end of alienation and inertia. Valid and authentic gathering at the table, then, is the goal of any process of reconciliation taken up by the church.

James Lopresti

I know too well the darker urges in myself,
the violence and selfishness.
I've seen little in him I can't recognize.
I also know my mind would shatter,
my soul would die if I did the things he does.
I'm tempted to believe there really is
a devil in him, some malefic,
independent force that makes him
less or other than a man.
That's too easy and too dangerous an answer;
it's how so many evils come to be.
I must reject, abhor, and fight against
these acts, and acknowledge that
they're not inhuman — just the opposite.
We can't separate the things
we do from what we are;
hate the sin and love the sinner is not
a concept I'll ever really understand.
I'll never love him — I'm not Christ.
But I'll try to achieve forgiveness,
because I know that in the end,
as always, Christ was right.

Terry Anderson

I T is a penance to work, to give oneself to others, to endure the pinpricks of community living. One would certainly say on many occasions: Give me a good thorough, frank, outgoing war, rather than the sneak attacks, stabs in the back, sparring, detracting, defaming, hand-to-hand jockeying for position that goes on in offices and "good works" of all kinds, another and miserably petty kind of war. St. Paul said that he "died daily." This too is penance, to be taken cheerfully, joyfully, with the hope that our own faith and joy in believing will strengthen Chuck and all the others in jail.

So let us rejoice in our own petty sufferings and thank God we have a little penance to offer. "An injury to one is an injury to all," the Industrial Workers of the World proclaimed. So an act of love, a voluntary taking on oneself of some of the pain of the world, increases the courage and love and hope of all.

Dorothy Day

I N the Christian view both sin and justification presuppose the effective revealing word of God: For our part, we must respond to God's word with a zeal both for the fear of God and for authentic divine existence, despite all "suppression." This zeal, in its turn, is due to previous grace. It is only in this way that we can have the right attitude toward our past and with a willingness which is itself a gratuitous gift allow God's revealing word to destroy in us pharisaic self-righteousness and convince us of sin.

Karl Rahner

FORGIVENESS breaks the chain of causality because the one who "forgives" you — out of love — assumes the consequences of what *you* have done. Forgiveness, therefore, always entails a sacrifice. The price you must pay for your own liberation through another's sacrifice is that you in turn must be willing to liberate in the same way, irrespective of the consequences to yourself.

Dag Hammerskjöld

THOSE who approach the sacrament of penance obtain pardon from God's mercy for the offense committed against God and are, at the same time, reconciled with the church which they have wounded by their sins and which by charity, by example and by prayer labors for their conversion.

Dogmatic Constitution on the Church

THE poor render us great service. Almsgiving atones for sins that we have not been able to wash away otherwise. What does Scripture say in this regard? "Water quenches a flaming fire, and alms atone for sins." The effects of almsgiving are similar to those of baptism; just as baptism remits sin, even so almsgiving atones for sins. Just as water extinguishes a fire, so does almsgiving extinguish sin; the fires of hell have been kindled for sin; almsgiving quenches them.

Jerome
Fifth century

HAPPY the pardoned,
whose sin is canceled,
in whom God finds
no evil, no deceit.

While I hid my sin,
my bones grew weak
from endless groaning.

Day and night,
under the weight of your hand,
my strength withered
as in a summer drought.

Then I stopped hiding my sin
and spoke out,
"God, I confess my wrong."
And you pardoned me.

No wonder the faithful
pray to you in danger!
Even a sudden flood
will never touch them.

You, my shelter,
you save me from ruin.
You encircle me
Psalm 32:2 – 7   with songs of freedom.

I am in charge of conversion, and I give understanding to all who experience conversion. Or does it not seem to you," he said, "that conversion itself is understanding? Conversion," he said, "is great understanding. The sinner understands that he or she has done evil in the sight of the Lord, awareness of the deed arises in the heart, but the sinner experiences conversion and no longer does evil but entirely good, and has a humbled and penitential spirit, because of the sin. So you see that conversion is great understanding."

The Shepherd of Hermas

EVERY endeavor to make peace between one person and another, or one nation and another, is worthy of our heartfelt admiration. Every sincere and eager movement toward peace, from whatever quarter it may come, provided that it conceal no deceit and be inspired by pure justice and universal love, any such movement, we repeat, is worthy of our trust and respect.

All is forgiven to those who know how to forgive and are willing to do so.

Pope John XXIII

WE owe it to each other to recognize that the ability to forgive can't be rushed. We do a great disservice to our families and friends when we rush forgiveness because, in fact, simple time may be all that's needed to foster it.

Doris Donnelly

Sᴵɴ is a spreading sickness of the spirit and demands prompt healing. To deal with it, we need a passion for communion, a passion so great that we will not fear the painful work of reconciliation. In this work, we shall need prayerful time, space and reflection to examine our wounds. We shall need grace and encouragement to search our hearts for the ways in which each of us involved is responsible for any separation. We shall need special grace so that the ceremony of reunion will not turn into another battleground for more pain and personal injury. We should always come to the peace table unarmed! We should approach reunion with a resolve not to reach back in history for a weapon of past offense, for some old hurt with which to hurl new pain at the other. From beginning to end, the prayer of reconciliation within our homes demands the presence of the All Holy One.

Edward Hays

Yᴇsᴛᴇʀᴅᴀʏ I was plundering the possessions of others; today I am giving away my own; almsgiving covers up greed. Happy the one whose sins are forgiven in baptism; second to baptism, however, penance is like a plank after shipwreck. The penitent, too, may thus be called happy.

Jerome
Fifth century

SINCE we possess Christ who is peace, we must put an end to this enmity and live as we believe he lived. He broke down the separating wall, uniting what was divided, bringing about peace by reconciling in his single person those who disagree. In the same way, we must be reconciled not only with those who attack us from outside, but also with those who stir up dissension within; flesh then will no longer be opposed to the spirit, nor the spirit to the flesh. Once we subject the wisdom of the flesh to God's law, we shall be re-created as one single person at peace. Then, having become one instead of two, we shall have peace within ourselves.

Gregory of Nyssa
Fourth century

WHY is it that it is often easier for us to confess our sins to God than to another? God is holy and sinless, God is a just judge of evil and the enemy of all disobedience. But another person is sinful as we are. The other knows from experience the dark night of secret sin. Why should we not find it easier to go to another than to the holy God? But if we do, we must ask ourselves whether we have not often been deceiving ourselves with our confession of sin to God, whether we have not rather been confessing our sins to ourselves and also granting ourselves absolution. And is not the reason perhaps for our countless relapses and the feebleness of our Christian obedience to be found precisely in the fact that we are living on self-forgiveness and not a real forgiveness? Self-forgiveness can never lead to a breach with sin; this can be accomplished only by the judging and pardoning Word of God itself.

Dietrich Bonhoeffer

IN fact, we frequently join together to commit injustice. It is thus only fitting that we should help each other in doing penance so that we who are freed from sin by the grace of Christ may work with all people of good will for justice and peace in the world.

Rite of penance

THIS is the love that resides in the self, the self-love, out of which all love pours. The fountain, the source. At the center. One gives up all the treasured sorrow and self-mistrust, all the precious loathing and suspicion, all the secret triumphs of withdrawal. One bends in the wind. There are many disciplines that strengthen one's athleticism for love. It takes all one's strength. And yet it takes all one's weakness too. Sometimes it is only by having all one's so-called strength pulverized that one is weak enough, strong enough, to yield. It takes that power of nature in one which is neither strength nor weakness but closer perhaps to *virtu*, person, personalized energy. Do not speak about strength and weakness, manliness and womanliness, aggressiveness and submissiveness. Look at this flower. Look at this child. Look at this rock with lichen growing on it. Listen to this gull scream as he drops through the air to gobble the bread I throw and clumsily rights himself in the wind. Bear ye one another's burdens, the Lord said, and he was talking law.

Love is not a doctrine. Peace is not an international agreement. Love and peace are beings who live as possibilities in us.

Mary Caroline
Richards

THE Blessed One said: "Though robbers or highwaymen might carve you limb from limb with a double-handed saw, yet even then whoever gives way to hatred is not a follower of my teaching. You should train yourselves like this: 'Our minds will not become deranged, we will not utter evil speech, we will remain with a friendly heart, devoid of hatred: and, beginning with these people, we will develop the thought of loving-kindness.'"

Majjhima Nikāya

THE bloodied cross is
but a propulsion
that pulls us
toward the margins,
toward the edges
of life.

Where, there,
outside the gates
of imagined respectability
we would join
the forgotten chosen
to walk them back,
as they lead us in,
to the center of
God's eye
and God's heart.

Jack McClure

RECONCILIATION is an intensely sought but elusive goal. Part of the difficulty is the sheer enormity of the task, so great that it seems well-nigh unachievable. For it is not only a matter of healing memories and receiving forgiveness, it is also about changing the structure in society that provoked, promoted and sustained violence.

Robert J. Schreiter

HUMAN beings fail and fail; and in the course of ordinary care a mother is all the time mending her failures. These relative failures with immediate remedy undoubtedly add up eventually to a communication, so that the baby comes to know about success. Successful adaptation thus gives a sense of security, a feeling of having been loved. As analysts we know about this because we are all the time failing, and we expect and get anger. If we survive we get used. It is the innumerable failures followed by the sort of care that mends that build up into a communication of love, of the fact that there is a human being there who cares. Where failure is not mended within the requisite time, seconds, minutes, hours, then we use the term *deprivation*. A deprived child is one who, after knowing about failures mended, comes to experience failure unmended. It is then the lifework of the child to provoke conditions in which failures mended once more give the pattern to life.

D. W. Winnicott

IT would not be right to make penance or other bodily
works either your motivation or your goal, for they are
only finite. They are done in time that comes to an end, and
sometimes one has to abandon them or have them taken
away. In fact, it would not only not be meritorious but
would offend me if you continued in these works when circumstances or obedience to authority made it impossible
to do what you had undertaken. So you see how finite they
are. Take them up, then, not as your goal but only as they
are useful. For if you take them as a goal and then have to
abandon them at some point, your soul will be left empty.

Catherine of Siena
Fourteenth century

LORD, let me return to you,
let me come to you,
reach out to me,
I am alone.
Alone.
Empty-hearted.
Afraid of myself.
Let me come to you.
Reach out to me.

Preparatory service for
the Days of Awe

By your cross, remove anger and put an end to war.
By your cross, eliminate strife and conflicts.
By your cross, calm disorders and pacify the angry.
By your cross, humble the proud,
expose the self-serving, and remove the enemy.
By your cross, curb violence and anger.
By your cross, establish your church in strength
and make her monasteries firm.
By your cross, let the priests be honorable
and the deacons reverent.
Sustain the elderly, subdue the haste of youth,
and rear the young.
By your cross, pardon sinners, forgive wrongdoers,
and guard your flock which now worships before you.
For your church glories in the sign of the cross.

Maronite liturgy   Save us and all your people.

One beautiful Irish image describes conversion as
"bending the knees of your heart."

Michael R. Prieur

Lord, give me a little while that I may cry, for I have heard
that tears accomplish much and can become a sufficient
Apocalypse of Sedrach   cure for the humble body of your creatures.

Y OU forgave the woman who repented,
show us also your mercy.

You brought back the lost sheep on your shoulders,
pity us and lead us home.

You promised paradise to the good thief,
take us with you into your Kingdom.

You died for us and rose again,
make us share in your death and resurrection.   Rite of penance

T HE people of God accomplishes and perfects continual
repentance in many different ways. It shares in the suffering of Christ by enduring its own difficulties, carries out
works of mercy and charity, and adopts ever more fully the
outlook of the gospel message. Thus the people of God
becomes in the world a sign of conversion to God.   Rite of penance

F ORGIVENESS is not the comfortable, often somewhat superior, "I forgive you" that comes so easily to human lips
when emotions have cooled. Things are then smoothed
over but the resentment descends into the unconscious
together with a hidden condition that the "forgiven" injury
shall not be repeated. The ultimate experience of forgiveness brings a change of heart, a *metanoia* of the spirit, after
which every seeming injury, injustice, rejection, past, present or future, every so-called blow of fate, becomes, as it
were, an essential note in the music of God, however dis-
cordant it may sound to our superficial hearing. And the
experience excludes nothing — which means that in this
moment of forgiveness all one's sins and weaknesses are
included, being at the same time both remembered and
known as the essential darkness which has revealed to us
the light.   Helen M. Luke

Francis de Sales
Seventeenth century

Sin is shameful only when we commit it; when it has been converted by confession and repentance it becomes honorable and salutary.

Where charity and love prevail
There God is ever found;
Brought here together by Christ's love
By love are we thus bound.

With grateful joy and holy fear
His charity we learn;
Let us with heart and mind and soul
Now love him in return.

Forgive us now each other's faults
As we our faults confess;
And let us love each other well

Ubi Caritas   In Christian holiness.

No sooner had the people rebelled against Moses than they repented and even asked him to pray for them, and he in turn did not hesitate to respond (Numbers 21:7). From this we learn both the humility of Moses and the power of repentance; and also that one who is being sincerely asked

Midrash   to forgive should not stay angry.

I F you forgive others their trespasses, your heavenly Father
will also forgive you; but if you do not forgive others, nei-
ther will your Father forgive your trespasses.   Matthew 6:14–15

I am alone in the dark, and I am thinking
what darkness would be mine if I could see
the ruin I wrought in every place I wandered
and if I could not be
aware of One who follows after me.
Whom do I love, O God, when I love Thee?
The great Undoer who has torn apart
the walls I built against a human heart,
the Mender who has sewn together the hedges
through which I broke when I went seeking ill,
the Love who follows and forgives me still.
Fumbler and fool that I am, with things around me
of fragile make like souls, how I am blessed
to hear behind me footsteps of a Savior!
I sing to the east; I sing to the west:
God is my repairer of fences, turning my paths into rest.   Jessica Powers

B LESS God, who forgives your sin
and heals every illness,
who snatches you from death
and enfolds you with tender care,
who fills your life with richness
Psalm 103:3 – 5   and gives you an eagle's strength.

A brother asked the abbot Pastor, saying, "I have sinned
a great sin, and I am willing to do penance for three
years." But the abbot Pastor said, "That is a great deal." And
the brother said, "Do you order me one year?" And again
the old man said, "That is a great deal." Some who stood
by said, "Up to forty days?" The old man said, "That is a
great deal." And then he added, "I think that if a man would
repent with his whole heart and would not reckon to do
Sayings of the   again that for which he now repents, God would accept a
Desert Fathers   penance of three days."

C HRISTIAN reconciling activity is God's reconciling
activity — not in the sense that what we do substitutes
now for what God would do, nor in the sense that God
approves of what we do and ratifies it as God's own, but in
the sense that there is a genuine co-doing in which God's
forgiving works in and through our forgiving and makes
Bernard Cooke   ours possible and effective.

S LOWLY turning, ever turning
From our lovelessness like ice,
From our unforgiving spirit,
From the grip of envy's vise,

Slowly turning, ever turning
Toward the lavish life of spring,
Toward the word of warmth and pardon,
Toward the mercy welcoming!

Slowly turning, ever turning
From our ego-centered gaze,
From our self-enclosing circle,
From our narrow, petty ways,

Slowly turning, ever turning
Toward the foreigner as friend,
Toward the city without ghetto, *
Toward the greatness without end!

Slowly turning, ever turning
From our fear of death and loss,
From our terror of the darkness
From our scorning of the cross,

Slowly turning, ever turning
Toward the true and faithful one,
Toward the light of daybreak dawning,
Toward the phoenix-risen sun!   Dolores Dufner

Leo the Great
Fifth century

Sins, not people, must be hated. The arrogant are to be corrected, the weak to be tolerated. And those who are to be more severely chastised are to be punished, not out of vindictiveness, but in the interest of healing.

Pope John Paul II

Convincing the world of the existence of sin is not the same as condemning it for sinning. "God did not send the Son into the world to condemn the world, but that the world might be saved through him." Convincing the world of sin means creating the conditions for its salvation. Awareness of our own sinfulness, including that which is inherited, is the first condition for salvation; the next is the confession of this sin before God who desires only to receive this confession so that God can save us. To save means to embrace and lift up with redemptive love, with love that is always greater than any sin. In this regard the parable of the prodigal son is an unsurpassable paradigm.

Rite of penance

We can only approach the Kingdom of Christ by *metanoia*. This is a profound change of the whole person by which one begins to consider, judge and arrange one's life according to the holiness and love of God, made manifest in his Son in the last days and given to us in abundance. The genuineness of penance depends on this heartfelt contrition. For conversion should affect persons from within so that it may progressively enlighten them and render them continually more like Christ.

Give all people the courage and valor to achieve peace and real disarmament. Give the church the courage to teach not how one can cleverly reconcile the egotism among us, but rather how in light of the folly of the cross one can and indeed must assume direct responsibility for unconditional justice and peace. Convert the hearts of the mighty so that they may not yield to the deceitful pursuit of power in order to justify their own actions, nor deceive themselves and others while claiming to serve the ends of peace by proliferating arms. And ultimately, teach us within our own lives to further the cause of peace unselfishly.   Karl Rahner

Never disappoint the trust
another puts in you.
Be warm and merciful
and let none go from you empty-handed.
The least you can offer
is your time and patience,
your affection and your prayer.

Rule for a New Brother

Our church stands firmly in the faith, although some have lapsed because they fear the loss of their outstanding positions or other personal sufferings. Although these have separated from us, we have not given them up; in the past we have urged them and now we continue to encourage them to do penance, in the hope that they may receive pardon from God who can give it; whereas if they were abandoned by us, they might become worse.

Cyprian
Third century

WE have inherited a story which needs to be told in such a way that the many painful wounds about which we hear day after day can be liberated from their isolation and be revealed as part of God's relationship with us. Healing means revealing that our human wounds are most intimately connected with the suffering of God. To be a living memory of Jesus Christ, therefore, means to reveal the connections between our small sufferings and the great story of God's suffering in Jesus Christ, between our little life and the great life of God with us. By lifting our painful forgotten memories out of the egocentric, individualistic, private sphere, Jesus Christ heals our pains. He connects them with the pain of all humanity, a pain he took upon himself and transformed. To heal, then, does not primarily mean to take pains away but to reveal that our pains are part of a greater pain, that our sorrows are part of a greater sorrow, that our experience is part of the great experience of him who said, "But was it not ordained that the Christ should suffer and so enter into the glory of God?"

Henri J. M. Nouwen

WHAT tasks of reconciliation are asked of me? I realize that reconciliation is the healing of broken relationships, the gentle persuasion of the alienated to reestablish their membership in the family of God. It is "coming home," learning to trust again. A basic part of reconciliation in [prison] is to offer to spiritual orphans a true home, a place where, in Robert Frost's words, "when you go there, they have to take you in." Reconciliation is bringing harmony to the cacophony of broken relationships which, like the noise in the cell units, is intensified by being enclosed. Reconciliation is recognizing the wounds of alienation and the pain of broken love relationships. It is the remedying of currents of hate in the prison's underground structure.

Pauline Grady

FURTHERMORE, correct one another, not in anger but in peace, as you find in the gospel; and if anyone wrongs his neighbor, let no one speak to him, nor let him hear a word from you, until he repents. As for your prayers and acts of charity, and all your actions, do them all just as you find it in the gospel of our Lord.

Didache

HEAR us, almighty Lord, show us your mercy, Sinners we stand here before you.

Jesus our Savior, Lord of all the nations,
Christ our Redeemer hear the prayers we offer,
Spare us and save us, comfort us in sorrow.

Word of the Father, Keystone of God's building,
Source of our gladness, Gateway to the Kingdom,
Free us in mercy from the sins that bind us.

God of compassion, Lord of might and splendor,
Graciously listen, hear our cries of anguish,
Touch us and heal us where our sins have wounded.

Humbly confessing that we have offended,
Stripped of illusions, naked in our sorrow,
Pardon, Lord Jesus, those your blood has ransomed.

Innocent captive, you were led to slaughter,
Sentenced by sinners when they brought false witness.
Keep from damnation those your death has rescued.

Attende Domine
Tenth century

BUT WHILE HE WAS STILL FAR OFF, HIS FATHER SAW HIM AND WAS
FILLED WITH COMPASSION; HE RAN AND PUT HIS ARMS AROUND
HIM AND KISSED HIM.   Luke 15:20

~

You must picture me alone in that room in Magdalen,
night after night, feeling, whenever my mind lifted even
for a second from my work, the steady, unrelenting
approach of him whom I so earnestly desired not to meet.
That which I greatly feared had at last come upon me. In
the Trinity Term of 1929 I gave in, and admitted that God
was God, and knelt and prayed: perhaps, that night, the
most dejected and reluctant convert in all England. I did not
then see what is now the most shining and obvious thing;
the divine humility which will accept a convert even on
such terms. The Prodigal Son at least walked home on his
own feet. But who can duly adore that love which will
open the high gates to a prodigal who is brought kicking,
struggling, resentful, and darting his eyes in every direction
for a chance to escape? The words *compelle intrare*, com-
pel them to come in, have been so abused by the wicked
that we shudder at them; but, properly understood, they
plumb the depth of divine mercy. The hardness of God is
kinder than the softness of people, and his compulsion is
our liberation.

C. S. Lewis

I have always overshadowed Jonas with my mercy. . . .
Have you had sight of me, Jonas my child? Mercy within
mercy within mercy.

Thomas Merton

ONE of the criminals who were hanged there kept derid-ing him and saying, "Are you not the Messiah? Save yourself and us!" But the other rebuked him, saying, "Do you not fear God, since you are under the same sentence of condemnation? And we indeed have been condemned justly, for we are getting what we deserve for our deeds, but this man has done nothing wrong." Then he said, "Jesus, remem-ber me when you come into your kingdom." He replied, "Truly I tell you, today you will be with me in Paradise."   Luke 23:39 – 43

THE foundation of mercy is in love, and the operation of mercy is our protection in love; and this was revealed in such a way that I could not perceive, without mercy's prop-erties, in any other way than as if it were all love in love.

That is to say, as I see it, mercy is a sweet, gracious opera-tion in love, mingled with plentiful pity, for mercy works, protecting us, and mercy works, turning everything to good for us. Mercy for love allows us to fail to a certain extent; and inasmuch as we fail, in so much we fall, and inasmuch as we fall, in so much we die. For we must necessarily die inasmuch as we fail to see and feel God, who is our life. Our failing is dreadful, our falling is shameful, and our dying is sorrowful. But yet in all this the sweet eye of pity is never turned away from us, and the operation of mercy does not cease.   Julian of Norwich
Fourteenth century

MAY almighty God have mercy on us,
forgive us our sins,
and bring us to everlasting life.

Roman rite

SATISFACTION must not be ruled out or absolution denied
to those who in time of necessity or in the moment of
pressing danger beg for the protection of penance followed
by absolution. For we cannot put limitations on the mercy
of God or set temporal limits for whom no delays in pardon are experienced when the conversion is genuine.

Leo the Great
Fifth century

I fear God no more; I go forward to wander forever in a
wilderness made of God's infinite mercy alone.

Jessica Powers

YOUR mercy, Lord, spans the sky;
your faithfulness soars among the clouds.
Your integrity towers like a mountain;
your justice runs deeper than the sea.
Lord, you embrace all life:
How we prize your tender mercy!

Psalm 36:6–8

Paul says rightly that it is God who brings about reconciliation, not us. Only God can truly understand the enormity of what has been done to us. And so our attention must remain on the consequences of the deed for the victim. God restores the humanity that has been ripped away from us. Victims experience this as a welling up of grace in their lives, a graciousness of trust and of love. It seems to come from nowhere. And it is a trust and a love with no strings attached. It says at once, "You are worth trusting with this grace. You are worth loving."

Robert J. Schreiter

The literature of illumination reveals this above all: Although it comes to those who wait for it, it is always, even to the most practiced and adept, a gift and a total surprise. I return from one walk knowing where the killdeer nests in the field by the creek and the hour the laurel blooms. I return from the same walk a day later scarcely knowing my own name. Litanies hum in my ears, my tongue flaps in my mouth Ailinon, alleluia!

Annie Dillard

But the great tenderness of the Lord has had mercy on you and your family, and will strengthen you and lay your foundations in his glory. You, however, do not get careless, but take heart and strengthen your family. For just as the smith hammering at his work prevails over the object as he wishes, so too the righteous word spoken daily prevails over all evil.

The Shepherd of Hermas

FATHER, all-powerful and ever-living God,
we praise and thank you through Jesus Christ our Lord
for your presence and action in the world.

In the midst of conflict and division,
we know it is you
who turn our minds to thoughts of peace.
Your Spirit changes our hearts:
enemies begin to speak to one another,
those who were estranged join hands in friendship,
and nations seek the way of peace together.

Your Spirit is at work
when understanding puts an end to strife,
when hatred is quenched by mercy,
and vengeance gives way to forgiveness.
For this we should never cease

Roman rite   to thank and praise you.

IT is not dutiful observance that keeps us from sin, but
something far greater: It is love. And this love is not something which we develop by our own powers alone. It is a
sublime gift of the divine mercy, and the fact that we live
in the realization of this mercy and this gift is the greatest

Thomas Merton   source of growth for our love and for our holiness.

THE quality of mercy is not strained,
It droppeth as the gentle rain from heaven
Upon the place beneath. It is twice blessed;
It blesseth him that gives, and him that takes,
'Tis mightiest in the mightiest, it becomes
The thronéd monarch better than his crown:
His sceptre shows the force of temporal power,
The attribute to awe and majesty,
Wherein doth sit the dread and fear of kings:
But mercy is above this sceptred sway,
It is enthronéd in the hearts of kings,
It is an attribute to God himself;
And earthly power doth then show likest God's,
When mercy seasons justice.

William Shakespeare
Seventeenth century

BUT should I still not be able to master my feelings, I will remember the words of the Buddha, "that this person too is the owner and heir of his deeds; that he is sprung from them, and that he will have his wholesome and unwholesome deeds as his inheritance." In this way I will overcome hatred and feel compassion.

Nyänatiloka

THERE is *always* something left to love. And if you ain't
learned that, you ain't learned nothing. Have you cried
for that boy today? I don't mean for yourself and for the
family 'cause we lost the money. I mean for him: what he
been through and what it done to him. Child, when do you
think is the time to love somebody the most? When they
done good and made things easy for everybody? Well then,
you ain't through learning — because that ain't the time at
all. It's when he's at his lowest and can't believe in hisself
'cause the world done whipped him so! When you starts
measuring somebody, measure him right, child, measure
him right. Make sure you done taken into account what
hills and valleys he come through before he got to wherever he is.

Lorraine Hansberry

THEREFORE, I tell you, her sins, which were many, have
been forgiven; hence she has shown great love. But the
one to whom little is forgiven, loves little."

Luke 7:47

LET us be practical and ask the question, How do we love
our enemies?

First, we must develop and maintain the capacity to forgive.
He who is devoid of the power to forgive is devoid of the
power to love. It is impossible even to begin the act of loving one's enemies without the prior acceptance of the
necessity, over and over again, of forgiving those who inflict
evil and injury upon us. It is also necessary to realize that
the forgiving act must always be initiated by the person
who has been wronged, the victim of some great hurt, the
recipient of some tortuous injustice, the absorber of some
terrible act of oppression. The wrongdoer may request forgiveness. . . . like the prodigal child. . . . But only the injured
neighbor, the loving parent back home, can really pour out
the warm waters of forgiveness.

Martin Luther King, Jr.

A N old man was asked by a certain soldier if God received a penitent man. And after heartening him with many words, he said to him at the last, "Tell me, beloved, if your cloak were torn, would you throw it away?" He said, "Nay, but I would patch it and wear it." The old man said to him, "If you would spare your garment, shall not God *Sayings of the* have mercy on God's own image?" *Desert Fathers*

R EMIND me ten times and more
    of all that you have forgiven me —
  without even waiting for my sorrow,
  the very instant that I slipped and sinned.

Remind me ten thousand times and more
    of your endless absolution,
    not even sorrow required on my part,
    so broad the bounty of your love.

Yes, I can — I will — forgive
    as you have forgiven me.   Edward Hays

Two days later, halfway through the service, it seemed as though Ruth was going to be the lone member of the bereaved family there. A female quartet from Linden Baptist Church had already sung "Abide with Me"; the wife of the mortician had read the condolence cards and the minister had launched into his "Naked came ye into this life and naked shall ye depart" sermon, which he had always believed suitable for the death of a young woman; and the winos in the vestibule who came to pay respects to "Pilate's girl," but who dared not enter, had begun to sob, when the door swung open and Pilate burst in, shouting, "Mercy!" as though it were a command. A young man stood up and moved toward her. She flung out her right arm and almost knocked him down. "I want mercy!" she shouted, and began walking toward the coffin, shaking her head from side to side as though somebody had asked her a question and her answer was no.

Halfway up the aisle she stopped, lifted a finger, and pointed. Then slowly, although her breathing was fast and shallow, she lowered her hand to her side. It was strange, the languorous limp hand coming to rest at her side while her breathing was coming so quick and fast. "Mercy," she said again, but she whispered it now. The mortician scurried toward her and touched her elbow. She moved away from him and went right up to the bier. She tilted her head and looked down. Her earring grazed her shoulder. Out of the total blackness of her clothes it blazed like a star. The mortician tried to approach her again, and moved closer, but when he saw her inky, berry-black lips, her cloudy, rainy eyes, the wonderful brass box hanging from her ear, he stepped back and looked at the floor.

"Mercy?" Now she was asking a question. "Mercy?"

It was not enough. The word needed a bottom, a frame. She straightened up, held her head high, and transformed the plea into a note. In a clear bluebell voice she sang it out — the one word held so long it became a sentence — and before the last syllable had died in the corners of the room, she was answered in a sweet soprano: "I hear you."

The people turned around. Reba had entered and was singing too. Pilate neither acknowledged her entrance nor missed a beat. She simply repeated the word "Mercy," and Reba replied. The daughter standing at the back of the chapel, the mother up front, they sang.

In the nighttime.
Mercy.
In the darkness.
Mercy.
In the morning.
Mercy.
At my bedside.
Mercy.
On my knees now.
Mercy. Mercy. Mercy. Mercy.

Toni Morrison

FROM the depths I call to you,
Lord, hear my cry.
Catch the sound of my voice
raised up, pleading.

Psalm 130:1–2

THERE is one church here, so I go to it. On Sunday mornings I quit the house and wander down the hill to the white frame church in the firs. On a big Sunday there might be twenty of us there; often I am the only person under sixty, and feel as though I'm on an archaeological tour of Soviet Russia. The members are of mixed denominations; the minister is a Congregationalist, and wears a white shirt. The man knows God. Once, in the middle of the long pastoral prayer of intercession for the whole world — for the gift of wisdom to its leaders, for hope and mercy to the grieving and pained, succor to the oppressed, and God's grace to all — in the middle of this he stopped, and burst out, "Lord, we bring you these same petitions every week." After a shocked pause, he continued reading the prayer. Because of this, I like him very much.

Annie Dillard

O God, be merciful to all who groan under the bondage of their sins, and show your grace to those who are burdened with the memory of their offenses; that, as not one of us is free from fault, so not one may be shut out from pardon.

Gelasian sacramentary

WHEN God saw the world falling to ruin because of fear, he immediately acted to call it back to himself with love. He invited it by his grace, preserved it by his love, and embraced it with compassion. When the earth had become hardened in evil, God sent the flood both to punish and to release it. He called Noah to be the father of a new era, urged him with kind words, and showed that he trusted him; he gave him fatherly instruction about the present calamity, and through his grace consoled him with hope for the future. But God did not merely issue commands; rather with Noah sharing the work, he filled the ark with the future seed of the whole world. The sense of loving fellowship thus engendered removed servile fear, and a mutual love could continue to preserve what shared labor had effected.

Peter Chrysologus
Fifth century

JESUS said, "Father, forgive them; for they do not know what they are doing."

Luke 23:34

God, again and again through the ages you have sent messengers
  To this pitiless world:
They have said, "Forgive everyone," they have said,
    "Love one another—
    Rid your hearts of evil."
They are revered and remembered, yet still in these dark
    days
We turn them away with hollow greetings, from outside
    the doors of our houses.

And meanwhile I see secretive hatred murdering the
    helpless
  Under cover of night;
And Justice weeping silently and furtively at power
    misused,
  No hope of redress.
I see the young working themselves into a frenzy,
In agony dashing their heads against stone to no avail.

My voice is choked today; I have no music in my flute:
  Black moonless night
Has imprisoned my world, plunged it into nightmare. And
    this is why,
  With tears in my eyes, I ask:
Those who have poisoned your air, those who have
    extinguished your light,
Can it be that you have forgiven them? Can it be that you
    love them?

Rabindranath Tagore

FORGIVENESS is hard because it involves loving other people in spite of the evil that they have done to us. When we forgive, we don't deny the hurt that we have received. We don't deny that it was wrong. We don't pretend that nothing happened. But we acknowledge that there is more to the offender than the offense. It's that *more* that we acknowledge when we forgive; it's that *more* that we love in spite of the offense.

Daniel E. Pilarczyk

COMPASSION wears Saturn's rings on the fingers of her left hand. She is intimate with the life force. She understands the meaning of sacrifice. She is not afraid to die. There is nothing you cannot tell her.

Compassion speaks with a slight accent. She was a vulnerable child, miserable in school, cold, shy, alert to the pain in the eyes of her sturdier classmates. The other kids teased her about being too sentimental, and for a long time she believed them. In ninth grade she was befriended by Courage.

Courage lent Compassion bright sweaters, explained the slang, showed her how to play volleyball, taught her you can love people and not care what they think about you.

In many ways Compassion is still the stranger, neither wonderful nor terrible, herself, utterly, always.

J-Ruth Gendler

As the first martyr prayed to you for his murderers, O Lord, so we fall before you and pray; forgive all who hate and maltreat us and let not one of them perish because of us, but may all be saved by your grace, O God the all-bountiful.

Orthodox liturgy

In Christ you give your people
a season of reconciliation and grace:
a time to draw new breath
for our journey back to you,
a time to open our hearts to your Spirit
and respond to the needs of all.

Roman rite

Fridfeldt sat down on the edge of the bed. He tried to talk with the sick man, but there was no sign of recognition. He bent over and shouted in the man's ear, but received no recognizable answer. Occasionally they could make out what the old man said, but he spoke of far-away, distant things, about rock blasting and oxen.

"Father was always such a good man," said the weeping daughter. "I know of course that he will have it better now, but it is so hard to part with him."

"When I got here," she continued after a moment, "I said, 'You are thinking about Jesus, are you not, Father?' And he answered me, 'I am not able to, Lena. I can't think any longer. But I know that Jesus is thinking of me.'"

Bo Giertz

I seek mercy
for the women stoned
and their accomplice—the darkness of the night,
for the scent of clover and the branches
on which they fell intoxicated
like quails and woodcocks,
for their second lives,
for their love torments,
unrelieved by compassion.
I seek mercy
for the moonlight and for the rubies,
of their skin,
for the moonlight's dusk,
for the showers of their undone hair,
for the handful of silvery branches,
for their loves naked
and damned—
for all Mary Magdalenes.

Desanka Maksimovic

Come, Lord,
and cover me with the night.
Spread your grace over us
as you assured us you would do.

Your promises are more than
all the stars in the sky;
your mercy is deeper than the night.
Lord, it will be cold.
The night comes with its breath of death.
Night comes; the end comes; you come.

Lord, we wait for you
Ghanaian prayer   day and night.

We like to imagine that peace is a delicate thing which
we must lock up within ourselves and protect and
hide in the depths of our hearts so that it may not be lost or
be evaporated. But in the scriptures peace is spoken of in
an utterly different way. There it is said that God's peace
is a mighty power, which of itself can keep our hearts and
Anders Nygren   our thoughts.

WITHOUT being forgiven, released from the consequences of what we have done, our capacity to act
would, as it were, be confined to one single deed from
which we could never recover; we would remain the victims
of its consequences forever, not unlike the sorcerer's appren-
tice who lacked the magic formula to break the spell.   Hannah Arendt

For you are God of the repenters.
And in me you will manifest all your grace;
and although I am not worthy,
    you will save me according to the multitude of your
        mercies.
Because of this I shall praise you continually
    through all the days of my life;
because all the hosts of heaven praise you,
    and sing to you forever and ever.   Prayer of Manasseh

INCOLN tried love and left for all history a magnificent drama of reconciliation. When he was campaigning for the presidency one of his archenemies was a man named Stanton. For some reason Stanton hated Lincoln. He used every ounce of his energy to degrade him in the eyes of the public. So deep-rooted was Stanton's hate for Lincoln that he uttered unkind words about his physical appearance, and sought to embarrass him at every point with the bitterest diatribes. But in spite of this Lincoln was elected President of the United States. Then came the period when he had to select his cabinet which would consist of the persons who would be his most intimate associates in implementing his program. He started choosing men here and there for the various secretaryships. The day finally came for Lincoln to select a man to fill the all-important post of the Secretary of War. Can you imagine whom Lincoln chose to fill this post? None other than the man named Stanton. There was an immediate uproar in the inner circle when the news began to spread. Adviser after adviser was heard saying, "Mr. President, you are making a mistake. Do you know this man Stanton? Are you familiar with all the ugly things he said about you? He is your enemy. He will seek to sabotage your program. Have you thought this through, Mr. President?" Mr. Lincoln's answer was terse and to the point: "Yes, I know Mr. Stanton. I am aware of all the terrible things he has said about me. But after looking over the nation, I find that he is the best man for the job." So Stanton became Abraham Lincoln's Secretary of War and rendered an invaluable service to his nation and his President. Not many years later Lincoln was assassinated. Many laudable things were said about him. Even today millions of people still adore him as the greatest of all Americans. H. G. Wells selected him as one of the six great men of history. But of all the great statements made about Abraham Lincoln, the words of Stanton remain among the greatest. Standing near the dead body of the man he once hated, Stanton referred to him as one of the greatest men that ever lived and said, "He now belongs to the ages." If Lincoln had hated Stanton both men would have gone to their graves as bitter enemies. But through the power of love Lincoln transformed an enemy into a friend. It was this same attitude that made it possible for Lincoln to speak a kind word about the South during the Civil War when feeling was most bitter. Asked by a shocked bystander how he could do this, Lincoln said, "Madam, do I not destroy my enemies when I make them my friends?" This is the power of redemptive love.   Martin Luther King, Jr.

THE days are surely coming, says the LORD, when I will make a new covenant with the house of Israel and the house of Judah. It will not be like the covenant that I made with their ancestors when I took them by the hand to bring them out of the land of Egypt—a covenant that they broke, though I was their husband, says the LORD. But this is the covenant that I will make with the house of Israel after those days, says the LORD: I will put my law within them, and I will write it on their hearts; and I will be their God, and they shall be my people. No longer shall they teach one another, or say to each other, "Know the LORD," for they shall all know me, from the least of them to the greatest, says the LORD; for I will forgive their iniquity, and remember their sin no more.

Jeremiah 31:31–34

I learned, I learned—when one might be inclined
To think, too late, you cannot recover your losses—
I learned something of the nature of God's mind,
Not the abstract Creator but the God who caresses
The daily and nightly earth; the One who refuses
To take failure for an answer till "again and again" is worn.

Patrick Kavanagh

THE crux of the matter is, of course, the question of forgiveness. Forgetting is something that time alone takes care of, but forgiveness is an act of volition, and only the sufferer is qualified to make the decision.

Simon Wiesenthal

Y OUR mercy, O God of all life, extends to all who live. You turn from our transgressions, that we may turn to you. For you love all beings, despising nothing that you have made. For how could you hate what you have established, and what would endure without your love? All things are touched by your grace, for they are yours. Lord, you take delight in life, for your eternal spirit dwells in all that breathes.

Preparatory service for the Days of Awe

T HE qualities of a good confessor are summarized . . . in the following jingle from a manual for curates in the diocese of Autun:

Let the priest hear confessions in an open place in
church:
At the faces of women not staring;
everyone patiently hearing;
pardon to supplicants promising;
bearable penances imposing.

In literary merit the translation is not much inferior to the original, and the teaching contained in it does not go much beyond the commonplaces of etiquette. Andreas de Escobar's rhymes are more explicit, as he tells us the confessor ought to be

soft in correcting
prudent in instructing
conscientious in punishing
courteous in questioning
discreet in imposing a penance
gentle in hearing the penitent
kind in absolving.

Thomas N. Tentler

ALL holy God,
how wonderful the work of your hands!
You restored the beauty of your image
when sin had scarred the world.

As a mother tenderly gathers her children,
you embraced a people as your own
and filled them with longing
for a peace that would last
and for a justice that would never fail.

Through countless generations
your people hungered for the bread of freedom.
From them you raised up Jesus, the living bread,
in whom ancient hungers were satisfied.
He healed the sick,
though he himself would suffer;
he offered life to sinners,
though death would hunt him down.
But with a love stronger than death,
he opened wide his arms

Proposed Eucharistic
Prayer   and surrendered his spirit.

Clearly, then, the gospel is not the proclamation of the "Bad News" that God wants to punish us, but rather the proclamation of the "Good News" that God chooses us to be his people in spite of the fact that we are sinners. Karl Barth expressed this idea beautifully when he said that God deals with us, not with a natural "therefore," but with a miraculous "nevertheless." The sequence is not: "We are unworthy, therefore God rejects us," but rather "We are unworthy, nevertheless God elects us."

William H. Shannon

Don't carry on a futile battle against yourself,
don't divide yourself into good and evil.
Resist the temptation to analyze yourself—
turn your attention to the Lord instead,
and be deeply receptive.
Accept yourself in God's light
and concentrate on the mission
you have to accomplish.

Rule for a New Brother

Forgiveness and compassion hold hands like sisters and call forth a strength that relies one on the other. Our actions and behavior are influenced by our security or lack of it, our frustrations, and usually our compulsions. We readily forgive a child, but we forget that growing up is a lifelong process. To understand that we each do the best we can with the maturity we have enables us to allow each other our inevitable "mistakes" and to practice the art of true forgiveness.

Noela N. Evans

THERE'S a wideness in God's mercy
Like the wideness of the sea;
There's a kindness in God's justice
Which is more than liberty.
There is plentiful redemption
In the blood that has been shed;
There is joy for all the members
In the sorrows of the head.

There is welcome for the sinner,
And a promised grace made good.
There is mercy with the Savior;
There is healing in his blood.
There is grace enough for thousands
Of new worlds as great as this;
There is room for fresh creations
In that upper home of bliss.

For the love of God is broader
Than the measures of the mind,
And the heart of the Eternal
Is most wonderfully kind.
If our love were but more simple,
We should take him at his word,
And our lives would be all sunshine
In the kindness of our Lord.

Troubled souls, why will you scatter
Like a crowd of frightened sheep?
Foolish hearts, why will you wander
From a love so true and deep?
There is welcome for the sinner,
And more graces for the good;
There is mercy with the Savior,
There is healing in the blood.

Frederick William
Faber

I once heard a young man talk about his life as a child in Cambodia. All of the children in his village spent years imprisoned in a barbed-wire encampment. Four times a day people were brought to the outskirts of that encampment to be killed. The children were all lined up and forced to watch. According to the rule, if one of them started to cry, then he or she would also be killed. This boy said that each time people were brought to be killed, he was absolutely terrified that among them would be a friend, neighbor or relative. He knew that if that happened, he would start to cry, and then he would be killed himself. He lived with this terror for years. He said that in that circumstance, the only way he could survive was to completely cut off all feeling, to dehumanize himself altogether.

After many years the political situation changed in Cambodia and this boy was adopted by an American family and brought to the United States. At that point in his life, he knew that now he would be able to survive only if he learned to love again, to break down the walls that he had been forced to create. The young man related that he learned to love again by looking into the eyes of his foster father and see-ing there so much love for him. In the mirror of his foster father's love, the boy realized that he was indeed lovable, and that therefore he was also capable of extending love.

Looking at people and communicating that they can be loved, and that they can love in return, is giving them a tremendous gift. It is also a gift to ourselves. We see that we are one with the fabric of life. This is the power of *metta:* to teach ourselves and our world this inherent loveliness.

Metta binds all beings together. Buddhist psychology iden-tifies it as the cohesive factor in consciousness. When a per-son experiences anger, the heart is dry. It becomes moist when that person feels love. When we put together two substances in nature that are dry, they cannot cohere; there is no way for them to join. When we add wetness, these two substances can bond; they can come together. In just the same way, the force of *metta,* lovingkindness, allows us to cohere, to come together within ourselves and with all beings. The beauty of this truth moved the Buddha to say that sustaining a loving heart, even for the duration of the snap of a finger, makes one a truly spiritual being.

Sharon Salzberg

YET it was I who taught Ephraim to walk,
    I took them up in my arms;
but they did not know that I healed them.
I led them with cords of human kindness,
    with bands of love.
I was to them like those
    who lift infants to their cheeks.
Hosea 11:3–4   I bent down to them and fed them.

YOU were speaking of the Last Judgment. Allow me to
laugh respectfully. I shall wait for it resolutely, for I have
Albert Camus   known what is worse: the judgment of men.

I T is tempting to think of the examination of conscience at the end of the day as a kind of score sheet — Visitors 5, Home 0 — to be entered into the heavenly ledger, with the end of time as a final grand and glorious reconciling of the human tally. And, as with all scores, it is tempting to settle some and contest others. "Yes, I did smack the baby's bottom, but it was only after . . ." and the argument commences. We uncover, in a strip-tease of the conscience, strategically, and then scramble to gather up and restore our covering. It is too fearsome to admit nakedness.

But nakedness is what we are, in truth, invited into in the examination of conscience. To learn in nakedness is to lie in nakedness, as one lies still under the soft, exploring touch of the beloved, and to reveal oneself — marked, flawed, scarred, misshapen — and begin to understand that the beloved alters not, withdraws never, when it alteration finds.

It is the image Jesus gives us of the prodigal son: ill-clad, ill-fed and having squandered all his father's gifts, embraced in his father's arms, standing close under his father's gaze. The son cannot conceal the toll of the road — its odor, its dusting of grit and streaky sheen of sweat — nor can he produce what he does not have, the lost fortune. With neither the means nor the strength for concealment, the son had to choose: To come at all was to come stripped and naked. Yet the Father does not withdraw or turn away. He sees, and loves.

Melissa Musick
Nussbaum

EVERYONE says forgiveness is a lovely idea, until they have something to forgive, as we had during the war. And then to mention the subject at all is to be greeted with howls of anger. It is not that people think this too high and difficult a virtue: It is that they think it hateful and contemptible. "That sort of talk makes them sick," they say. And half of you already want to ask me, "I wonder how'd you feel about forgiving the Gestapo if you were a Pole or a Jew?"

So do I. I wonder very much. Just as when Christianity tells me that I must not deny my religion even to save myself from death by torture, I wonder very much what I should do when it came to the point. I am not trying to tell you . . . what I could do—I can do precious little—I am telling you what Christianity is. I did not invent it. And there, right in the middle of it, I find "Forgive us our sins as we forgive those that sin against us." There is no slightest suggestion that we are offered forgiveness on any other terms. It is made perfectly clear that if we do not forgive we shall not be forgiven. There are no two ways about it. What are we to do?

It is going to be hard enough, anyway, but I think there are two things we can do to make it easier. When you start mathematics you do not begin with calculus; you begin with simple addition. In the same way, if we really want (but all depends on really wanting) to learn how to forgive, perhaps we had better start with something easier than the Gestapo. One might start with forgiving one's husband or wife, or parents or children, or the nearest NCO, for something they have done or said in the last week. That will probably keep us busy for the moment. And secondly, we might try to understand exactly what loving your neighbor as yourself means. I have to love him as I love myself. Well, how exactly do I love myself?

Now that I come to think of it, I have not exactly got a feeling of fondness or affection for myself, and I do not even always enjoy my own society. So apparently "Love your neighbor" does not mean "feel fond of him" or "find him attractive." . . . I can look at some of the things I have done with loathing and horror. So apparently I am allowed to loathe and hate some of the things my enemies do. Now that I come to think of it, I remember Christian teachers telling me long ago that I must hate a bad man's actions, but not hate the bad man: or, as they would say, hate the sin but not the sinner.

For a long time I used to think this a silly, straw-splitting distinction: How could you hate what a man did and not hate the man? But years later it occurred to me that there was one man to whom I had been doing this all my life — namely myself. However much I might dislike my own cowardice or conceit or greed, I went on loving myself. There had never been the slightest difficulty about it. In fact, the very reason why I hated the things was that I loved the man. Just because I loved myself, I was sorry to find that I was the sort of man who did those things. Consequently Christianity does not want us to reduce by one atom the hatred we feel for cruelty and treachery. We ought to hate them. Not one word of what we have said about them needs to be unsaid. But it does want us to hate them in the same way in which we hate things in ourselves: being sorry that the man should have done such things, and hoping, if it is anyway possible, that somehow, sometime, somewhere, he can be cured and made human again.   C. S. Lewis

I F one has received an injury, then, even if the wrongdoer has not asked for forgiveness, the receiver of the injury must nevertheless ask God to show the wrongdoer compassion, even as Abraham prayed to God for Abimelech and Job prayed for his friends. Rabbi Gamaliel said: Let this be a sign to you, that whenever you are compassionate, the Compassionate One will have compassion on you.

The Talmud

T HE biblical writers even speak of the anger of God against whatever outrages God's righteousness, but God is not content to be angry or to destroy — God moves toward costly reconciliation. For Christians too, indignation, struggle, conflict are sometimes right, but they can be only stages on the way to the ultimate goal of reconciliation. Still, they may be necessary stages if that reconciliation is not to be superficial, but a really deep coming together.

John Macquarrie

I N the name of God, the Merciful, the Compassionate, praise be to God, Lord of the worlds, the Merciful, the Compassionate, in whose hand is the day of judgment. It is you we worship, you we ask for aid. Guide us along the right path, the path of those you bless, not of those who incur your anger, nor that of those who go astray.   The Koran

L AMB of God, you take away the sin of the world,
   have mercy on us.
Lamb of God, you take away the sin of the world,
   have mercy on us.
Lamb of God, you take away the sin of the world,
   grant us peace.   Roman rite

THEN THE SON SAID TO HIM, "FATHER, I HAVE SINNED AGAINST HEAVEN AND BEFORE YOU; I AM NO LONGER WORTHY TO BE CALLED YOUR SON." BUT THE FATHER SAID TO HIS SLAVES, "QUICKLY BRING OUT A ROBE — THE BEST ONE — AND PUT IT ON HIM; PUT A RING ON HIS FINGER AND SANDALS ON HIS FEET."

Luke 15:21 – 22

~

WAY back in the room, Sergeant Espinoza was taking the stairsteps one at a time. Looking fiercely in their direction. But Atticus was past caring about that future; that was only government and paperwork. His shifty second son was there, found and alive, and if there was hurt in his face and he seemed to have visited every room in hell, it hardly mattered now; Atticus was flooded with joy. He'd had his mind set on just the one thing and got surprised by the far better. "Will you forgive me?" Scott had said. Words wouldn't half do it, so Atticus hugged his son hard against himself. Wanting to fill him up with his love.

Ron Hansen

For a Catholic, ritual confession, or the sacrament of reconciliation, as it is called now, is an emotional ceremony, no matter how informal the setting. This was my first confession in twenty-five years, my first formal step back to the church. I'd spent months wrestling with myself; months trying to understand where that moment in an English church six months ago was taking me; more months lying chained on a cot with nothing to do but examine myself, study the Bible and try to deal, alone, with my anger, frustration, remorse. This smiling, soft-spoken priest, also a hostage, dressed like me in white cotton shorts and T-shirt, frightened, in his own pain and anger received the full flood of my emotions, guilts and concerns, returning warmth, love and understanding.

By the end of our session, the bare floor around us is littered with crumpled tissues. Both he and I are crying. Finally, I kneel beside him. "Father, forgive me, for I have sinned, in word and in thought, in what I have done and what I have not done."

He rests his right hand lightly on my head. "In the name of a gentle, loving God, you are forgiven." He pulls my head gently to his shoulder and hugs me.

Terry Anderson

So, if I go on to confess, not what I was, but what I am, the good that comes of it is this. There is joy in my heart when I confess to you, yet there is fear as well; there is sorrow, and yet hope. But I confess not only to you but also to all believers; all who share my joy and all who, like me, are doomed to die; all who are my fellows in your kingdom and all who accompany me on the pilgrimage, whether they have gone before or are still to come or are with me as I make my way through life.

Augustine of Hippo
Fifth century

A little girl came to her first confession and began by chatting about her mom and dad, her new puppy, the classes she loved, a recent vacation . . . she could hardly be stopped. Finally the priest intervened: "Would you like to say a little word about your sins?" She retorted: "That's getting kinda personal!"

Kathleen Hughes

I pardon all things. I ignore many things in the zeal and pledge of gathering together the community. Even those things which have been committed against God, I examine not with the full judgment of religion. I myself am almost negligent in remitting sins much more than I ought. I embrace with prompt and full love those returning with repentance, confessing their sin with simple and humble satisfaction.

Cyprian
Third century

MILLY yearned to absolve all those who had troubled her in her life. She forgave her father for naming her Milly instead of Jo Ann, and her mother for passing on to her genes that made her oversensitive to small hurts and slights. She forgave her brother for reading her diary, and her sister for her pretty legs, and her cat for running in front of a truck and winding up pressed flat as a transfer on the road. She forgave everyone who had ever forgotten her birthday and everyone who looked over her shoulder at parties for some- one more attractive to talk to. She forgave her boss for being waspish and her lover for lack of empathy and her husband for making uncalled-for remarks about stale break- fast cereal and burned toast.

All this dispensing of absolution emptied Milly out and made her light as air. She had a sensation of floating, of weightlessness, and it seemed to her that bells were chim- ing inside her head.

Carol Shields

I will sprinkle clean water upon you, and you shall be clean from all your uncleannesses, and from all your idols I will cleanse you. A new heart I will give you, and a new spirit I will put within you; and I will remove from your body the heart of stone and give you a heart of flesh. I will put my spirit within you, and make you follow my statutes and be careful to observe my ordinances. Then you shall live in the land that I gave to your ancestors; and you shall be my people, and I will be your God.

Ezekiel 36:25–28

But with regard to penitents who are doing penance for graver or for lesser sins, the practice of the Roman church is that they be forgiven on the Thursday before Easter, so long as no illness intervenes. Moreover, it belongs to the bishop to discern seriousness of sins, so that he may listen attentively to the penitent's confession and to the weeping and tears of the one making amendment, and order him to be released only when he has given evidence of fitting satisfaction. Of course, if one should become ill, even to the point of despair for his life, he must be released before Easter, lest he depart this world without communion.

Innocent I
Fifth century

Tertullian
Third century

This external act, rather expressively designated by the Greek word for it in common use, is the *exomologesis.* Herein we confess our sin to the Lord, not as though God were ignorant of it, but because satisfaction receives its proper determination through confession, confession gives birth to penitence and by penance God is appeased.

Rescue me before I am caught by my persecutors
For just as a little child who is afraid flees to her
    father,
and the father, stretching out his hands, snatches her off
    the ground,
and puts his arms around her,
and the child clasps her hands around her father's neck,
and regains her breath after her fear,
and rests at her father's breast,
the father, however, smiles at the confusion of her childish
    mind,
likewise you too, Lord, stretch out your hands upon me
    as a child-loving father,

Joseph and Aseneth   and snatch me off the earth.

I came to Mass today
to hide in Latin words
and smell the dust of ritual.
I came for sanctuary
where the powerful and poor
together kneel
and unstoppable time
holds still
like a snapshot in the eye of God.
I came to a place without lessons,
where no one is distilling truth
like Tennessee whiskey.
I came to float like a flower
in a Japanese pool.
I came
for the veins under my skin
to swell like the virgin in Nazareth
and burst wine.
I came for something
you cannot get over the counter.
I came because justice
will not happen before cocktails.
I came because my child's cold
did not gather in her chest
like a summer storm.
I came
because in my nightmare chases
I wake to sweat
the moment before capture.
I came
because I want it to be true
that I will go in peace
when this Mass is ended.

John Shea

Wɪᴛʜ a cry for mercy the liturgy begins, in the litany of "Lord, have mercy." With a cry for mercy the service of the word concludes, as we pray for all the world's needy. With a cry for mercy we assemble at the table to claim the bread broken for us. "Mercy," we cry at the beginning, middle and end. Mercy is the womb we enter when we worship together. I think of the pilgrimage church at the monastery of Taizé, France: While all our home churches are busy repainting walls gleaming white and installing powerful light fixtures and designing spaces of brightness, the Taizé church embraces us with a merciful round darkness. It is too dark to read, but we are encircled with votive lights as with a palpable mercy. All the pilgrims, all the languages, all the denominations, all the ages sit there on the unlit floor, themselves walking bodies of need, settled now into divine compassion, in, under, around, through.

Gail Ramshaw

Iɴ our culture it often seems a mark of professionalism to be impervious to others' pain. Sometimes this is a good thing: I would prefer that my surgeon operate with eyes not blurred with tears! Yet in some areas we have gone too far, and, along with their own woundedness, our healers deny the reality of others' suffering. Spiritual directors are not professionals, but amateurs who aspire to reflect Christ's love. So we take sin and pain upon ourselves, not in grandiose self-promotion, but because the assumption of such a burden is one of the risks of hospitality.

Margaret Guenther

THE sixteenth-century Reformers, and after them the Lutheran and Reformed Churches, asserted that the practice of confession was both well-founded and profitable. Pastors at their consecration still promise to "keep secret those confessions which may be made for the quieting of conscience."

Max Thurian

A pastoral administrator from the West tells the story that one day an elderly priest showed up at the parish house, just off the interstate near a gas station where he had been getting some gas. The middle-aged woman answered the door, and the priest asked if he could see a priest, because he wanted to go to confession. The woman explained that she was the administrator, and there was no priest in residence. The closest parish with a resident priest was seventeen miles away. The elderly priest seemed a little uncertain, so she invited him in for a cup of coffee. She had just baked some cookies, so she brought him to the kitchen, gave him some fresh-baked cookies and a cup of coffee, and he began to talk. After a while he mentioned how he had not been happy with his confession over the past few years, and really felt the need for something different, something deeper. He spoke on while she listened. Finally, after almost an hour of talking, confessing, praying, reading scripture and sharing cookies and coffee, the woman prayed the prayer from Mass: "May almighty God have mercy on us, forgive us our sins and bring us to everlasting life." He said, "Amen." She continued, "May the almighty and merciful Lord grant us pardon, absolution and remission of our sins." Again he said, "Amen," and then they embraced in a heartfelt sign of peace. As he was leaving, she offered him directions to the nearest parish with a resident, but he shook his head no, saying, "That's not necessary now, thank you; you did the trick!"

Edward Foley

JUST as baptism is a necessary sacrament, so is penance. And baptism, through being a necessary sacrament, has a twofold minister: the one whose duty it is to baptize in virtue of his office, namely, the priest, and another to whom the conferring of baptism is committed, in a case of necessity. In like manner the minister of penance, to whom, in virtue of his office, confession should be made, is a priest; but in a case of necessity even a layperson may take the place of a priest, and hear a person's confession.

Thomas Aquinas
Thirteenth century

THE ministry of the church is quite simple and adequately described by St. Paul as "the ministry of reconciliation" (2 Corinthians 5:18). This ministry of reconciliation, he declares, is given by God to those who themselves have been reconciled to him through Christ. This implies that the ministry of reconciliation belongs to the whole church. All Christians are, in a sense, ministers; and indeed, if Christ himself is the servant of the Lord and the agent of God's reconciling work, and if to be a Christian means to be conformed to Christ, then clearly every Christian shares in Christ's own ministry of service.

John Macquarrie

THEY asked the abbot Macarius, saying, "How ought we to pray?" and the old man said, "There is no need of much speaking in prayer, but often stretch out your hands and say, 'Lord, as you will and as you know, have mercy upon me.' But if there is war in your soul, add, 'help me.' And because God knows what we have need of, God shows us mercy."

Sayings of the
Desert Fathers

Pore soul!" murmured Mandy. She put Grandma's feet in the tub and, crouching beside it, slowly, slowly rubbed her swollen legs. Mandy was tired, too. Mrs. Harris sat in her nightcap and shawl, her hands crossed in her lap. She never asked for this greatest solace of the day; it was something that Mandy gave, who had nothing else to give. If there could be a comparison in absolutes, Mandy was the needier of the two — but she was younger. The kitchen was quiet and full of shadow, with only the light from an old lantern. Neither spoke. Mrs. Harris dozed from comfort, and Mandy herself was half asleep as she performed one of the oldest rites of compassion.

Willa Cather

Jesus cried with a loud voice, "Lazarus, come out!" The dead man came out, his hands and feet bound with strips of cloth, and his face wrapped in a cloth. Jesus said to them, "Unbind him, and let him go."

John 11:43–44

What, then, we read concerning Lazarus we ought to believe of every sinner who is converted, who, though he may have been stinking, nevertheless is cleansed by the precious ointment of faith. For faith has such grace that there where the dead stank the day before, now the whole house is filled with good odor.

Ambrose of Milan
Fourth century

African American
spiritual

THERE is a balm in Gilead to make the wounded whole;
There is a balm in Gilead to heal the sin-sick soul.

O Jesus, my feet are dirty. Come even as a slave to me, pour water into your bowl, come and wash my feet. In asking such a thing I know I am overbold, but I dread what was threatened when you said to me, "If I do not wash your feet I have no fellowship with you." Wash my feet then, because I long for your companionship. And yet, what am I asking? It was well for Peter to ask you to wash his feet, for him that was all that was needed to be clean in every part. With me it is different, though you wash me now I shall still stand in need of that other washing, the cleansing you promised when you said, "There is a baptism I must needs be baptized with."

Origen
Third century

LORD Jesus,
you chose to be called the friend of sinners.
By your saving death and resurrection
free me from my sins.
May your peace take root in my heart
and bring forth a harvest
of love, holiness and truth.

Rite of penance

THE scribes and the Pharisees brought a woman who had been caught in adultery; and making her stand before all of them, they said to him, "Teacher, this woman was caught in the very act of committing adultery. Now in the law Moses commanded us to stone such women. Now what do you say?" They said this to test him, so that they might have some charge to bring against him. Jesus bent down and wrote with his finger on the ground. When they kept on questioning him, he straightened up and said to them, "Let any one among you who is without sin be the first to throw a stone at her." And once again he bent down and wrote on the ground. When they heard it, they went away, one by one, beginning with the elders; and Jesus was left alone with the woman standing before her, "Woman, where are they? Has no one condemned you?" She said, "No one, sir." And Jesus said, "Neither do I condemn you. Go your way, and from now on do not sin again."

John 8:3 – 11

FORGIVENESS is a strong woman, tender and earthy and direct. Since her children have left home, she has embarked on an extended walking tour, visiting ruins and old monuments, bathing in rivers and hot springs, traveling through the small towns and large pulsing cities, tracing the current of sorrow under the stories she hears. Sometimes the city authorities and officials don't want her within their gates. If the people want her there enough, she always manages to find a way inside.

Forgiveness brings gifts wherever she goes. Simple ones, a three-stranded twig with leaves turning yellow, a belt she wove on an inkle loom, a little song that grows inside you and changes everything. She brought me a silver ring from the South with a pale stone, pink with a hint of brown. When I had asthma, she taught me how to breathe.

J-Ruth Gendler

Wᴇ must sit down
and reason together.
We must sit down:
men standing want to hold forth.
They rain down upon faces lifted.
We must sit down on the floor
on the earth
on stones and mats and blankets.
There must be no front to the speaking
no platform, no rostrum,
no stage or table.
We will not crane
to see who is speaking.
Perhaps we should sit in the dark.
In the dark we could utter our feelings.
In the dark we could propose
and describe and suggest.
In the dark we could not see who speaks
and only the words
would say what they say.
No one would speak more than twice.
No one would speak less than once.
Thus saying what we feel and what we want,
what we fear for ourselves and each other
into the dark, perhaps we could begin
to begin to listen.

Perhaps we should talk in groups
the size of new families,
not more, never more than twenty.
Perhaps we should start by speaking softly.
The women must learn to dare to speak,
The men must learn to bother to listen.
The women must learn to say I think this is so.
The men must learn to stop dancing solos on the ceiling.
After each speaks, she or he
will say a ritual phrase:
It is not I who speaks but the wind.
Wind blows through me.
Long after me, is the wind.

Marge Piercy

B UT I cannot achieve contemplation, as some can; and so, having to face and forgive my own failures, I have learned from them both the necessity and wonder of ritual. For ritual allows those who cannot will themselves out of the secular to perform the spiritual, as dancing allows the tongue-tied man a ceremony of love.

Andre Dubus

How do you know if you have forgiven? You tend to feel sorrow over the circumstance instead of rage, you tend to feel sorry for the person rather than angry. You tend to have nothing left to remember to say about it all. You understand the suffering that drove the offense to begin with. You prefer to remain outside the milieu. You are not waiting for anything. You are not wanting anything. There is no lariat snare around your ankle stretching from way back there to here. You are free to go. It may not have turned out to be a *happily ever after,* but most certainly there is a now a fresh *Once upon a time* waiting for you from this day forward.

Clarissa Pinkola Estés

But in Hades won't we pay the penalty for crimes committed here, either ourselves or our children's children?" "My friend," the young man will say as he does his calculation, "mystery rites have great power and the gods have great power of absolution. The greatest cities tell us this, as do those children of the gods who have become poets and prophets."

Plato
Fourth century BCE

Forgiveness is and always has been an impractical, illogical and uncommon approach to life: forgiving our enemies, doing good to those who hurt us, repaying evil with kindness. Contrary to myth, forgiveness is not instinctive, and most of the time it is a very difficult and time-consuming enterprise.

Doris Donnelly

ON Passover eve, Jewish custom advocates searching for old bread crumbs scattered in the crevices of the kitchen pantry, then tossing them into a paper sack and even burning them the next morning as a tangible display of springtime new beginnings. If, then, you find your life polluted by relationships going bad, toss out the anger that you bring to the table of life, the way you would last year's stale bread crumbs. Try actually writing down the habits that harm you and your family and literally burning them, the way Jews burn old bread crumbs, as your spiritual housecleaning this Easter.

Then later, as Easter Sunday brings you the Good News of Christian tradition, reflect on the fact that Jesus and his disciples once kept a Passover seder, at which time they would have pondered the seder's liturgical question: "Why is this night different from all other nights?" With the Easter Vigil just behind you, you might look at the faces of those you love, and know why this time is different. It will be the absence of destructive behavior patterns that you burned as the leaven of your soul. And you will look into the eyes of the people you love, recognizing that you have just left your own Egyptian bondage far behind.

Lawrence A. Hoffman

IN the last minutes he said more to her
Almost than in all their life together.
"You'll be in New Row on Monday night
And I'll come up for you and you'll be glad
When I walk in the door . . . Isn't that right?"
His head was bent down to her propped-up head.
She could not hear but we were overjoyed.
He called her good and girl. Then she was dead,
The searching for a pulsebeat was abandoned
And we all knew one thing by being there.
The space we stood around had been emptied
Into us to keep, it penetrated
Clearances that suddenly stood open.

Seamus Heaney   High cries were felled and a pure change happened.

MYTHICALLY, forgiveness can even be imagined as what
Joseph Campbell refers to as a "mask of God."
Something serves as such a mask if it inspires awe, situates
us in the cosmos, locates us socially in relation to each other,
and interprets for us who we are psychologically. Whenever
forgiveness awes us, or helps us know our place in creation,
or connects us to one another, or interprets us to ourselves,
we are meeting God, wearing one of the divine masks. It is
a God who grants forgiveness in relation to the way we grant
forgiveness and whose inner being (if one can speak of God's
Sally Harmony   psychology) is not only to grant, but to be, forgiveness.

OUR Father, we have wandered
And hidden from your face;
In foolishness have squandered
Your legacy of grace.
But now, in exile dwelling,
We rise with fear and shame,
As distant but compelling,
We hear you call our name.

And now at length discerning
The evil that we do,
Behold us, Lord, returning
With hope and trust to you.
In haste you come to meet us
And home rejoicing bring,
In gladness there to greet us
With calf and robe and ring.

O Lord of all the living,
Both banished and restored,
Compassionate, forgiving
And ever caring Lord,
Grant now that our transgressing,
Our faithlessness may cease.
Stretch out your hand in blessing
In pardon and in peace.

Kevin Nichols

THE main question today is not "Why have people stopped going to confession?" Rather we need to ask, "How can we most effectively respond to the reconciling Spirit of Christ alive in society?" The church will be effective to the degree that we see anew how God's kingdom, centered on reconciliation, is present in the whole world.

Robert J. Hater

THE soul is kissed by God
in its innermost regions.

With interior yearning,
grace and blessing
are bestowed.

It is a yearning to take on God's
gentle yoke,
it is a yearning to give one's self
to God's way.

Hildegard of Bingen
Twelfth century

THE sacrament of penance cannot be renewed except in the broader context of community renewal. Baptism and eucharist are the two basic and most important sacraments of reconciliation — both of them have as primary objectives the upbuilding of the Christian community. Can penance have any other purpose? The people of God have a God-given inalienable right to experience a community of loving concern. It seems to follow with absolute logic that our chief means of restoring the sacrament of reconciliation to its proper role is the prior restoration of the Sunday eucharistic liturgy as the primal sacrament of mutual reconciliation, as the regular experience of becoming one body because we eat the one bread.

Godfrey Diekmann

So when you are offering your gift at the altar, if you remember that your brother or sister has something against you, leave your gift there before the altar and go; first be reconciled to your brother or sister, and then come and offer your gift.

Matthew 5:23 – 24

THE highest adoration we offer to God "in spirit and in truth" is in this sharing of the breath of the Divine Spirit with one another in pardon and in love. That is why we are told to forgive our brother before we go to offer sacrifice. That is why we exchange the kiss of peace before communion. The kiss of peace is in some way part of our eucharistic communion; it symbolizes the spiritual sharing of the Holy Spirit. With a holy kiss we give the Holy Spirit to our brother, as if the flame of one candle were transferred to enlighten another.

Thomas Merton

THE sacrament whose nature and purpose is reconciliation cannot be convincingly and effectively celebrated in a church regarded as neglecting to reach out to challenge, support and reconcile those who are alienated from it. That, it seems, is the real crisis of penance.

James Dallen

IN the cross we recognize the ultimate sign of human rebellion and failure transformed into the sign of pardon and peace. Because it proclaims the parable of the cross, the sacrament of reconciliation can take both sin and grace with full seriousness. Personal sins *are* serious; they are a concrete acting out of that asphyxiating hostility that makes us empty and impotent when we are challenged to love. But grace is serious, too. For grace is God acting out in us, God giving us his own name: freedom.

Nathan Mitchell

GOD of unimaginable power and undying brilliance, look kindly upon the wondrous sacrament of your entire church, and bring about the salvation of the human family as the accomplishment of your constant convenantal love; and let the entire world see for itself that those whom life has cast down now stand tall and those who have grown stiff with age have their youth renewed, and in the end reconcile all through him from whom all have their beginning, Jesus Christ, your Son, our Lord.

Missal of Pius V

O God, beneath whose eyes every heart trembles and
all consciences are afraid, be favorable to the com-
plaints of all and heal the wounds of everyone, that just as
none of us is free from guilt, so none may be a stranger to
pardon, through our Lord Jesus Christ.

Gelasian sacramentary

D EARLY beloved, let us beseech the almighty and merciful God who desires not the death of sinners, but that
they be converted and live, that this your servant, making
amends unto true pardon, be accorded the pardon of mercy;
if there are any wounds which he has received from all his
offenses after the wave of the sacred bath, in this public
confession of his misdeeds may they be so healed that no
signs of the scars remain. Through our Lord Jesus Christ.

Medieval penitential
handbook

I T is necessary that you rejoice, because your brother had
been dead, and has come back to life; he had been lost
and has been found.

Pontificale
Romanum III

AND GET THE FATTED CALF AND KILL IT, AND LET US EAT AND
CELEBRATE. Luke 15:23

~

AFTER situating herself on a huge flat-sided rock, Baby Suggs bowed her head and prayed silently. The company watched her from the trees. They knew she was ready when she put her stick down. Then she shouted, "Let the children come!" and they ran from the trees toward her.

"Let your mothers hear you laugh," she told them, and the woods rang. The adults looked on and could not help smiling.

Then "Let the grown men come," she shouted. They stepped out one by one from among the ringing trees.

"Let your wives and children see you dance," she told them, and groundlife shuddered under their feet.

Finally she called the women to her. "Cry," she told them. "For the living and the dead. Just cry." And without covering their eyes the women let loose.

It started that way: laughing children, dancing men, crying women and then it got mixed up. Women stopped crying and danced; men sat down and cried; children danced, women laughed, children cried until, exhausted and riven, all and each lay about the clearing damp and gasping for breath. In the silence that followed, Baby Suggs, holy, offered up to them her great big heart.

She did not tell them to clean up their lives or to go and sin no more. She did not tell them they were the blessed of the earth, its inheriting meek or its glorybound pure.

She told them that the only grace they could have was the grace they could imagine. That if they could not see it, they would not have it.

"Here," she said, "in this here place, we flesh; flesh that weeps, laughs; flesh that dances on bare feet in grass. Love it. Love it hard. Yonder they do not love your flesh. They despise it. They don't love your eyes; they'd just as soon pick em out. No more do they love the skin on your back. Yonder they flay it. And O my people they do not love your hands. Those they only use to tie, bind, chop off and leave empty. Love your hands! Love them. Raise them up and kiss them. Touch others with them, pat them together, stroke them on your face 'cause they don't love that either. *You* got to love it, *you!* And no, they ain't in love with your mouth. Yonder, out there, they will see it broken and break it again. What you say out of it they will not heed. What you scream from it they do not hear. What you put into it to nourish your body they will snatch away and give you leavins instead. No, they don't love your mouth. *You* got to love it. This is flesh I'm talking about here. Flesh that needs to be loved. Feet that need to rest and to dance; backs that need support; shoulders that need arms, strong arms I'm telling you. And O my people out yonder, hear me, they do not love your neck unnoosed and straight. So love your neck; put a hand on it, grace it, stroke it and hold it up. And all your inside parts that they'd just as soon slop for hogs, you got to love them. The dark, dark liver — love it, love it, and the beat and beating heart, love that too. More than eyes or feet. More than lungs that have yet to draw free air. More than your life-holding womb and your life-giving private parts, hear me now, love your heart. For this is the prize.   Toni Morrison

Now the silence,
Now the peace,
Now the empty hands uplifted;
Now the kneeling,
Now the plea,
Now the Father's arms in welcome;
Now the hearing,
Now the pow'r,
Now the vessel brimmed for pouring;
Now the body,
Now the blood,
Now the joyful celebration;
Now the wedding,
Now the songs,
Now the heart forgiven leaping;
Now the Spirit's visitation,
Now the Son's epiphany,
Now the Father's blessing.
Jaroslav J. Vajda   Now. Now. Now.

A little boy was telling his aunt about his first communion and everything that would lead up to it. "There is this other thing first," he said, but then he drew a blank. "It's called . . . it's called . . . it's called First Relaxation!"

Barbara Quinn

Life drawn from the eucharist
makes all kinds of demands on you
to proclaim the meaning and greatness of this mystery.
You are called especially
to give the sacrament its full effect
in unity, community and service.
The unity of all Christians
and all people
must be closest to your heart.
Always and everywhere you are called
to rise above oppositions and divisions
in the universal love of Christ.
Always look for what unites
and fight everything that estranges and separates
one from another.

Rule for a New Brother

During his stay in Mezritch, the rav of Kolbishov saw an old man come to the Great Maggid and ask him to impose penance on him for his sins. "Go home," said the maggid. "Write all your sins down on a slip of paper and bring it to me." When the man brought him the list, he merely glanced at it. Then he said, "Go home. All is well." But later the rav observed that Rabbi Baer read the list and laughed at every line. This annoyed him. How could anyone laugh at sins!

For years he could not forget the incident, until once he heard someone quote a saying of the Baal Shem: "It is well known that no one commits a sin unless the spirit of folly possesses him. But what does the sage do if a fool comes to him? He laughs at all this folly and while he laughs, a breath of gentleness is wafted through the world. What was rigid, thaws, and what was a burden becomes light." The rav reflected. In his soul he said: "Now I understand the laughter of the holy maggid."

Martin Buber

O mild Christ,
the long plank table is spread with wealth
and everyone is gathered. The father puts aside
the quarrel with his one remaining son, the mother
wipes an eye on her apron, the daughters hush,
the cousins cease their cruel competition.
On the table, the brass centerpiece is heaped
with the brilliant red beads of pyracantha,
thorn of fire, torn from a low shrub beside the house;
and lifted above them — emblem of peace, emblem
        of affection —
the fleshy leaves of mistletoe, bearing its few pearls,
its small inedible berry.

Ellen Bryant Voigt

BEFORE sin, our life was eucharistic, for "eucharist" is the
only relationship between God and humankind which
transcends and transforms our created condition. This condition is that of a total, an absolute dependence. Dependence
is slavery. But when the dependence is accepted and lived
as "eucharist," i.e. as love, thanksgiving, adoration, it is no
longer dependence; it is an attitude of freedom, a state in
which God is the content of life.

Alexander
Schmemann

Seventy times seven God,
we come to confess
that often our lives fall
like smashed tablets to holy ground.
We say we will love
yet we manipulate.
We say we will dialogue
yet we dominate.
We say, "Speak truth!"
yet we hide in lie.
But the frustration of Paul
that the good we would, we do not
and the evil we should not, that we do
yields to the arms of the old man on the hill
who meets the self-hating scripts of the hired hands
with the robes of sonship
and the rings of daughterhood.
You are the father of parties
and no one outruns your joy.

Jesus told us
that for you
it is as easy to say walk
as to say forgive.
Say them both to us,
that we may walk in forgiveness.

John Shea

THE older we get, the greater becomes our inclination to give thanks, especially heavenwards. We feel more strongly than we could possibly have felt before that life is a free gift, and receive every unqualifiedly good hour in gratefully reaching out hands, as an unexpected gift.

But we also feel, again and again, an urge to thank our brothers and sisters, even if they have not done anything special for us. For what, then? For really meeting me when we met; for opening your eyes, and not mistaking me for someone else; for opening your ears, and listening carefully to what I had to say to you; indeed, for opening up to me what I really want to address — your securely locked heart.

Martin Buber

I'D love to see this place at dawn," Myra said suddenly. "That is always such a forgiving time. When that first cold, bright streak comes over the water, it's as if all our sins were pardoned; as if the sky leaned over the earth and kissed it and gave it absolution."

Willa Cather

I say, clap hands and let's come together in this meeting
    ground,
I say, clap hands and let's deal with each other with love,
I say, clap hands and let us get from the low road of
    indifference.
Clap hands, let us come together and reveal our hearts,
Let us come together and revise our spirits,
Let us come together and cleanse our souls,
Clap hands, let's leave the preening
And stop impostering our own history.
Clap hands, call the spirits back from the ledge,
Clap hands, let us invite joy into our conversation,
Courtesy into our bedrooms,
Gentleness into our kitchen,
Care into our nursery.
The ancestors remind us, despite the history of pain
We are a going-on people who will rise again.
And still we rise.

                                                   Maya Angelou

THE celebration of reconciliation is thus always an act in
    which the church proclaims its faith, gives thanks to
God for the freedom with which Christ has made us free,
and offers its life as a spiritual sacrifice in praise of God's
glory, as it hastens to meet the Lord Jesus.

                                                   Rite of penance

Out of what door that came ajar in heaven
drifted this starry manna down to me,
to the dilated mouth both hunger given
and all satiety?

Who bore at midnight to my very dwelling
the gift of this imperishable food?
my famished spirit with its fragrance filling,
its savor certitude.

The mind and heart ask, and the soul replies
what store is heaped on these bare shelves of mine?
The crumbs of the immortal delicacies
fall with precise design.

Mercy grows tall with the least heart enlightened,
and I, so long a fosterling of night,
here feast upon immeasurably sweetened
wafers of light.

Jessica Powers

Christ urges you, when you ask forgiveness for yourself,
to be especially generous to others, so that your actions
may commend your prayer.

Ambrose of Milan
Fourth century

AND we sinners have much cause for joy, if we but stop to think what is being proclaimed, realized and celebrated in the ritual of reconciliation. God, steadfastly faithful as always in spite of our severe provocations, summons us to repent of our sins; Christ, whose life was totally dedicated to calling sinners to repentance, calls us again; the spirit of God who was poured into our hearts at baptism for the forgiveness of sins and whom we celebrated in confirmation, moves us to repent and be forgiven; the church, wounded by our sins, offers us forgiveness and reconciliation; and moved by these loving gestures, we repent, are forgiven and are reconciled. There is cause enough for joy, cause enough for celebration. That celebrations are always better when shared with others is just one more reason for a genuinely communal celebration of penance.   Michael Lawler

NEVER be misled by the thought
that after failing and sinning
there can be no forgiveness.
Look critically at your own shortcomings,
but be sure that with the Lord
there is always abundance of redemption.

Your spiritual life must be mobile;
travel from oasis to oasis.
Yet the Lord can prepare a table
even in the desert,
and in the furnace of trial   *Rule for a New*
He will be coolness and refreshment.   *Brother*

Love bade me welcome; yet my soul drew back,
        Guilty of dust and sin.
But quick-eyed Love, observing me grow slack
        From my first entrance in,
Drew nearer to me, sweetly questioning
        If I lack'd anything.

'A guest,' I answer'd, 'worthy to be here:'
        Love said, 'You shall be he.'
'I, the unkind, ungrateful? Ah, my dear,
        I cannot look on Thee.'
Love took my hand and smiling did reply,
        'Who made the eyes but I?'

'Truth, Lord, but I have marr'd them: let my shame
        Go where it doth deserve.'
'And know you not,' says Love, 'Who bore the blame?'
        'My dear, then I will serve.'
'You must sit down,' says Love, 'and taste my meat.'
        So I did sit and eat.

George Herbert
Seventeenth century

We cry mercy as we gather around the table for the bread and wine; mercy, as the bread is broken; mercy, as friend and stranger commune; mercy also for me. But this is not like private confession and absolution, in which the word comes specifically to me. This mercy is for all, and for me as part of the all. The body of Christ "for you" is a plural you, you all, not the "for you, Suzie" that one hears these days. The table trains us in the habit of mercy by serving up mercy to all equally, each one of us—whether we know it or not—as needy as the next. Communion ought to train us to such mercy even when the table has been cleared, mercy we now are to share with one another through the week.

Gail Ramshaw

I tell you, there will be more joy in heaven over one sinner who repents than over ninety-nine righteous persons who need no repentance.

Luke 15:7

L ET us sing alleluia here on earth, while we still live in anxiety, so that we may sing it one day in heaven in full security. Why do we now live in anxiety? Can you expect me not to feel anxious when I read: *Is not our life on earth a time of trial?* Can you expect me not to feel anxious where there are so many temptations here below that prayer itself reminds us of them when we say: *Forgive us our trespasses, as we forgive those who trespass against us?* Every day we make our petitions, every day we sin. Do you want me to feel secure when I am daily asking pardon for my sins, and requesting help in time of trial? Because of my past sins I pray: *Forgive us our trespasses, as we forgive those who trespass against us,* and then, because of the perils still before me, I immediately go on to add: *Lead us not into temptation.* How can all be well with people who are crying out with me: *Deliver us from evil?* And yet while we are in the midst of this evil, let us sing alleluia to the good God who delivers us from evil.

Even here amidst trials and temptations let us, let all people sing alleluia. *God is faithful,* says holy scripture, *and he will not allow you to be tried beyond your strength.* So let us sing alleluia even here on earth.

Augustine of Hippo
Fifth century

FOR THIS SON OF MINE WAS DEAD AND IS ALIVE AGAIN; HE WAS
LOST AND IS FOUND.   Luke 15:11 – 24

~

Yes to one   is often no to another
here walks my grief   and here has often been
my peak of anguish   yes is the one need
of my whole life   but time and time again
law forces no   up through my heart and lips
spiked leaden ball   rending as it arises
leaving its blood and pain   yes is the soft
unfolding of petals   delicate with surprises
curve and caress   and billowing delight
out to the one or many   I would guess
heaven for me   will be an infinite
flower of one species   a measureless sheer
Jessica Powers   beatitude of yes

A changed way of life is a *consequence* of being forgiven,
not a *precondition* of forgiveness. Similarly, forgiveness
is not earned through penance; rather, penance ought to be
a response, a deep sign of gratitude, for having been forgiven. Thus, forgiveness is sustained through gratitude and
perfected in joy; in this sense, the surest sign of forgiveness
Paul J. Wadell   is a transformed life.

From now on, therefore, we regard no one from a human point of view, even though we once knew Christ from a human point of view; we know him no longer in that way. So if anyone is in Christ, there is a new creation: everything old has passed away; see, everything has become new! All this is from God, who reconciled us through Christ, and has given us the ministry of reconciliation; that is, in Christ God was reconciling the world to himself, not counting their trespasses against them, and entrusting the message of reconciliation to us. So we are ambassadors for Christ, since God is making his appeal through us; we entreat you on behalf of Christ, to be reconciled to God. For our sake he made him to be sin who knew no sin, so that in him we might become the righteousness of God.

2 Corinthians 5:16 – 21

We struggled against one another: now we are
        reconciled to struggle for one another.
We believed it was right to withstand one another: now
        we are reconciled to understand one another.
We endured the power of violence: now we are
        reconciled to the power of tolerance.
We built irreconcilable barriers between us: now we seek
        to build a society of reconciliation.
We suffered a separateness that did not work: now we are
        reconciled to make togetherness work.
We believed we alone held the truth: now we are
        reconciled in the knowledge that truth holds us.

South African national
service of thanksgiving

I once heard a liturgist say that just because the liturgy is in our language doesn't mean that we understand the language of the liturgy. The "Lord, have mercy" is a classic example. We hear those words and we believe that it is about tearing hair and beating bosom. Actually it is a translation of the Greek "Kyrie eleison." And the only people that I think understand the term properly are some group of very old black women somewhere in a small town in South Carolina. Go to one of the women and say, "Miz Jones?" "Yes, honey!" "Miz Jones, you have just won 13.5 million dollars in the lottery." Her response said in exultation and with hand raised would be to shout: "Lord, have mercy!" She knows "Kyrie eleison!"

J-Glenn Murray

WHAT gift can ever repay
God's gift to me?
I raise the cup of freedom
as I call on God's name!
I fulfill my vows to you, Lord,
standing before your assembly.

Psalm 116:12–14

THE green of Jesus
is breaking the ground
and the sweet
smell of delicious Jesus
is opening the house and
the dance of Jesus music
has hold of the air and
the world is turning
in the body of Jesus and
the future is possible

Lucille Clifton

MOTHERING Presence
enfold me
unfold me
and walk with me
and walk with me.

   I need to turn to you.
   I need to walk with you.
   I need to rest in you.

Beloved, come to me
but not to win my wars.
Beloved, come to me
but not to make my peace.
Come, O Loved One,
but not to build my house.

   If only you will walk with me.
   If only you will be with me.
   If only you will shelter me.

Maker of arithmetic
Weaver of number-worlds
Redeemer of equalities
Mother of odd/Sister of even
Creator of Aleph/Author of Bet:

   If only you will walk with me.
   If only you will shelter me.
   If only you will be with me.

Preparatory service for
the Days of Awe

LORD, today you made us known to friends
     we did not know,
And you have given us seats in homes
          which are not our own.
You have brought the distant near,
And made a brother of a stranger,
Forgive us Lord . . .

Polynesian prayer   We did not introduce you.

FOR in Christ all the fullness of God was pleased to dwell,
     and through him God was pleased to reconcile to him-
self all things, whether on earth or in heaven, by making
peace through the blood of his cross.

And you who were once estranged and hostile in mind,
doing evil deeds, he has now reconciled in his fleshly body
through death, so as to present you holy and blameless and
Colossians 1:19–22   irreproachable before him.

O God, I fear Thee not because
     I dread the wrath to come: for how
can such affright, when never was
A Friend more excellent than Thou?

Thou knowest well the heart's design,
The secret purpose of the mind,
And I adore Thee, light divine,
Abū-l-Husain al-Nūrī   Lest lesser lights should make me blind.

THEY had not the language; they had not the ideas; they had to discover everything. They had only one fact, and that was that *it had happened.* Messiah had come, and been killed, and risen; and they had been dead "in trespasses and sin," and now they were *not.* They were re-generate; so might everyone be. "The promise," they called to the crowd at Jerusalem, "is to you, and to your children, and to all that are afar off." "Repent and be baptized, every one of you, in the name of Jesus Christ for the remission of sins, and ye shall receive the Holy Ghost." They had believed in Jesus of Nazareth, without very clearly understanding him; his resurrection had seemed to justify them; but much more now they were justified, or rather he was justified. The thing had happened. In every kind of way it was true that the God of Israel would not leave their souls in hell nor suffer his Holy One to see corruption.

Charles Williams

THE spirit of the Lord GOD is upon me,
   because the LORD has anointed me;
he has sent me to bring good news to the oppressed,
   to bind up the brokenhearted,
to proclaim liberty to the captives,
   and release to the prisoners;
to proclaim the year of the LORD's favor,
   and the day of vengeance of our God;
   to comfort all who mourn;
to provide for those who mourn in Zion—
   to give them a garland instead of ashes,
the oil of gladness instead of mourning,
   the mantle of praise instead of a faint spirit.
They will be called oaks of righteousness,
   the planting of the LORD to display his glory.
They shall build up the ancient ruins,
   they shall raise up the former devastations;
they shall repair the ruined cities,
   the devastations of many generations.

Isaiah 61:1–4

THIS Prodigal Son is every human being: bewitched by the temptation to separate ourselves from the Father in order to lead an independent existence; disappointed by the emptiness of the mirage which had fascinated us; alone, dishonored, exploited when we try to build a world all for ourselves; sorely tried, even in the depths of our own misery, by the desire to return to communion with our Father. Like the father in the parable, God looks out for the return of the child, embraces us when we arrive and orders the banquet of the new meeting with which the reconciliation is celebrated.

The most striking element of the parable is the father's festive and loving welcome of the returning son: It is a sign of the mercy of God who is always willing to forgive. Let us say at once: reconciliation is principally a gift of the heavenly Father.

Reconciliation and
Penance
Pope John Paul II

THE Prophet says: "Lord, in your light we shall see the light." This is an overflowing light, enlightening every one who comes into the world. It shines upon everyone, the bad as well as the good, just as the sun shines upon all creatures. If they are blind to it, so much the worse for them. If we find ourselves in a darkened house, we need only sufficient light to find a window. Then we can open it and put our head out and we are in the light and become witnesses to the light.

Johannes Tauler
Fourteenth century

B UT now in Christ Jesus you who once were far off have been brought near by the blood of Christ. For he is our peace; in his flesh he has made both groups into one and has broken down the dividing wall, that is, the hostility between us. He has abolished the law with its commandments and ordinances, that he might create in himself one new humanity in place of the two, thus making peace, and might reconcile both groups to God in one body through the cross, thus putting to death that hostility through it. So he came and proclaimed peace to you who were far off and peace to those who were near; for through him both of us have access in one Spirit to the Father.

Ephesians 2:13–18

G OD's act of reconciliation in Christ does not merely absolve sins, it frees persons from the sinful mode of existence that makes them slaves to hostility and helplessness. It liberates people not only from failure and guilt but also from the suffocating goodness and virtue through which we attempt to earn salvation. The gospel of forgiveness is God's ultimate word of freedom uttered in the face of humanity's frantic effort to justify itself.

Nathan Mitchell

M Y heart begs for you, Lord:
hear me, so I can keep faith.
I beg you, make me free,
so I can live your laws.

Psalm 119:145–146

COME, you who are angry,
and make peace with your enemies.
Bow your head before them and embrace them.
Engrave in yourself the sign of the Son of God
as he humbled himself before others,
so humble yourself!

O disciple who shows anger toward your neighbor,
look for another Lord than the crucified One.
Those who show anger, not love, toward the neighbor
are against the Lord.

O disciple who seeks to imitate the Lord,
come and see how Christ humbled himself
and, like him, seek humility.
He gave you the command of pardon
and gave the keys of pardon
to the head of the disciples.

O merciful One, you destroyed anger;
Through your blood you established peace
between the inhabitants of heaven and earth.
By your good news,
you made all people brothers and sisters.

Maronite liturgy   Glory and praise to the Trinity.

THAT'S the difficulty in these times: ideals, dreams and
cherished hopes rise within us, only to meet the horri-
ble truth and be shattered.

It's really a wonder that I haven't dropped all my ideals,
because they seem so absurd and impossible to carry out.
Yet I keep them, because in spite of everything I still believe
Anne Frank   that people are really good at heart.

OOKING down into my father's
dead face for the last time
my mother said without
tears, without smiles
without regrets
but with civility
"Good night, Willie Lee, I'll see you
in the morning."
And it was then I knew that the healing
of all our wounds
is forgiveness
that permits a promise
of our return
at the end.

Alice Walker

HIS is how God acts—like the man searching for his lost
sheep, like the woman tirelessly sweeping for her lost
coin. Jesus thus images God as a woman searching for one
of her ten coins, looking for money that is terribly important to her. In telling the parable of the woman desperately
searching for her money, Jesus articulates God's own concern, a concern that determines Jesus' own praxis for table
community with sinners and outcasts. The parable then
challenges the hearer: Do you agree with the attitude of
God expressed in the woman's search for her lost "capital?"

Elisabeth Schüssler
Fiorenza

THERE are many words of God, and we all know them. We need not go farther to look for them; for since our youth we have been taught how to understand the living God through them. But the greatest word which crowns all the others is still this one, "I make all things new!" This word very particularly lends itself to being a support and a comfort if we become aware of how fleeting our life is and how quickly everything passes away and becomes dust and ashes. *All things new!* This is God who cannot tolerate what is corrupt and destructive but wants to repair it. Into this comfort of the living God we are allowed to enter and want to enter now.

R. Lejeune

I like the game called Sardines. In Sardines the person who is It goes and hides, and everybody goes looking for him. When you find him, you get in with him and hide there with him. Pretty soon everybody is hiding together, all stacked in a small space like puppies in a pile. And pretty soon somebody giggles and somebody laughs and everybody is found.

Medieval theologians even described God in hide-and-seek terms, calling him *Deus Absconditus*. But me, I think old God is a Sardine player. And will be found the same way everybody gets found in Sardines — by the sound of laughter of those heaped together at the end.

Robert Fulghum

FINDING ourselves; renewing ourselves. And realizing that because we have faced brokenness and come through it dancing and rejoicing, *we* are today's prophets. *We* are today's messengers bringing good news to the world. Transforming is the step where we recognize that the past is alive in the present. Transforming is the step where we gather up the richness of previous centuries and previous steps and offer that richness to the world.

Maria Harris

TWO weeks ago another 17-year old boy was shot dead in a drive-by shooting. Tragically, he was murdered just when his parish priest was helping him fill out application papers for Boys Town. Before the funeral Mass, his mother asked to speak to the congregation. She said, "I have no worries for my son; he is with God." But she was concerned about all of us. We must live not in violence and death but in peace and understanding. In order to achieve this goal, she said, we must forgive one another. She recognized that forgiveness had to start with herself, and for that reason she announced that she had forgiven the person who murdered her son. What a powerful beginning to the Mass of resurrection.

Charles W. Dahm

YOUR holiness shall consist of being truly human, not angelic. God has plenty of angels.

Kotsker Rebbe

ALL my life I never care what people thought bout nothing I did, I say. But deep in my heart I care about God. What he going to think. And come to find out, he don't think. Just sit up there glorying in being deef, I reckon. But it ain't easy, trying to do without God. Even if you know he ain't there, trying to do without him is a strain.

I is a sinner, say Shug. Cause I was born. I don't deny it. But once you find out what's out there waiting for us, what else can you be?

Sinners have more good times, I say.

You know why? she ast.

Cause you ain't all the time worrying bout God, I say.

Naw, that ain't it, she say. Us worry bout God a lot. But once us feel loved by God, us do the best us can to please him with what us like.

You telling me God love you, and you ain't never done nothing for him? I mean, not go to church, sing in the choir, feed the preacher and all like that?

But if God love me, Celie, I don't have to do all that. Unless I want to. There's a lot of other things I can do that I speck God likes.

Like what? I ast.

Oh, she say. I can lay back and just admire stuff. Be happy. Have a good time.

Well, this sound like blasphemy sure nuff.

She say, Celie, tell the truth, have you ever found God in church? I never did. I just found a bunch of folks hoping for him to show. Any God I ever felt in church I brought in with me. And I think all the other folks did too. They come to church to *share* God, not find God.

Alice Walker

THE tradition that past communities of faith have shaped can, in our hands, continue to grow. For the time, there is tension; sometimes between old sacramental habits and new sacramental attitudes, sometimes between the pastoral implications of sacramental theology and canonical requirements, always between human inertia and the call of Christ's Spirit. The need for reconciliation—on many levels—is, for the believer, Christ's challenge to his church to be converted, and the support that is needed to meet that challenge is present in his Spirit. In every case, the power of that Spirit, reconciling us to God in Christ, offers both challenge and support. A sense of how that Spirit has worked in the community of faith to shape our tradition gives us confidence to continue the work of sacramental reform and renewal as well as that of conversion and reconciliation. The future of a reconciling community is ours to shape.   James Dallen

I am a frayed and nibbled survivor in a fallen world, and I am getting along. I am aging and eaten and have done my share of eating too. I am not washed and beautiful, in control of a shining world in which everything fits, but instead am wandering awed about on a splintered wreck I've come to care for, whose gnawed trees breathe a delicate air, whose bloodied and scarred creatures are my dearest companions, and whose beauty beats and shines not *in* its imperfections but overwhelmingly in spite of them, under the wind-rent clouds, upstream and down.   Annie Dillard

I shall die, but that is all that I shall do for Death.

I hear him leading his horse out of the stall; I hear the
clatter on the barn-floor.
He is in haste; he has business in Cuba, business in the
Balkans, many calls to make this morning.
But I will not hold the bridle while he cinches the girth.
And he may mount by himself: I will not give him a leg up.

Though he flick my shoulders with his whip, I will not tell
him which way the fox ran.
With his hoof on my breast, I will not tell him where the
black boy hides in the swamp.
I shall die, but that is all that I shall do for Death; I am
not on his payroll.

I will not tell him the whereabouts of my friends nor of
my enemies either.
Though he promise me much, I will not map him the
route to any man's door.
Am I a spy in the land of the living, that I should deliver
men to Death?
Brother, the password and the plans of our city are safe
with me; never through me
Edna St. Vincent Millay   Shall you be overcome.

A ND then all that has divided us will merge
And then compassion will be wedded to power
And then softness will come to a world that is harsh and
    unkind
And then both men and women will be gentle
And then both women and men will be strong
And then no person will be subject to another's will
And then all will be rich and free and varied
And then the greed of some will give way to the needs of
    many
And then all will share equally in the Earth's abundance
And then all will care for the sick and the weak and the
    old
And then all will nourish the young
And then all will cherish life's creatures
And then all will live in harmony with each other and the
    Earth
And then everywhere will be called Eden once again   Judy Chicago

Notes

Excerpts from the English translation of *The Roman Missal* © 1973, International Committee on English in the Liturgy, Inc. (ICEL); excerpts from the English translation of *Rite of Penance* © 1974, ICEL; excerpts from the English translation of non-biblical readings from *The Liturgy of the Hours* © 1974, ICEL; excerpts from the English translation of *Eucharistic Prayers for Masses of Reconciliation* © 1975, ICEL; text of "Hear Us, Almighty Lord," "Our Father, We Have Wandered," "Lord Jesus, As We Turn from Sin," "We Sinned," and "Father of Mercy" From the *Resource Collection of Hymns and Service Music for the Liturgy* © 1981, ICEL; text of Eucharistic Prayer A © 1986, ICEL; the English translation of Psalms 13, 22, 25, 32, 36, 51, 103, 116, 119, 123, 130, 139 and 143 from the *Liturgical Psalter* © 1994, ICEL; excerpts from the English translation of *The Sacramentary* (Revised Edition) © 1994, ICEL. All rights reserved.

Scripture texts are from the *New Revised Standard Version Bible*, © 1989, by the Division of Christian Education of the National Council of Churches of Christ in the United States of America. Used by permission. All rights reserved.

(1) **Recently the newspapers:** *A Concise History of Preaching* by Paul Scott Wilson, © 1992. Reprinted by permission of Abingdon Press.

When was I ever: "The Death of a Hired Man" by Robert Frost. Public domain.

Milton was right: *The Great Divorce* by C. S. Lewis. Used by permission of HarperCollins, Ltd.

Original sin is: *The Fire and the Rose Are One* by Sebastian Moore, © 1981. Published by Seabury Press.

I read it in your word: *Poems from the Book of Hours* by Rainier Maria Rilke, tr. by Babette Deutch. © 1941, New Directions Publishing Corp. Used by permission of the publisher.

He did not: *Final Payments* by Mary Gordon, © 1978. Used by permission of Alfred A. Knopf, Inc.

The men and women: *Gates of Forgiveness*, © 1993, Central Conference of American Rabbis. Used by permission.

There can be: *Reconciliation: The Continuing Agenda*, Robert J. Kennedy, ed. Used by permission of The Liturgical Press.

A moral principle: *Amish Society*, Second (Revised) Edition, by John A. Hostettler, © 1963, 1968, The Johns Hopkins University Press.

The Buddha: *Lovingkindness: The Revolutionary Art of Happiness* by Sharon Salzberg, © 1995. Used by arrangement with Shambhala Publications, Inc., Boston.

Let us intercede: *The Apostolic Fathers*, 2nd ed., 1992, published by Baker Book House.

Each of you: *On the Pulse of Morning* by Maya Angelou. © 1993, Maya Angelou. Used by permission of Random House, Inc.

For in every: *The Way of Suffering* by Jerome A. Miller. Used by permission of Georgetown University Press.

Of all qualities: *Gates of Forgiveness*, © 1993, Central Conference of American Rabbis. Used by permission.

Lady of Silences: "Ash Wednesday," *Collected* (9) *Poems 1909-1962*, by T.S. Eliot. © 1936, Harcourt Brace & Company, © 1964, 1963, T.S. Eliot. Used by permission of the publisher.

A certain Timothy: *The Desert Fathers*, tr. from the Latin with an Introduction by Helen Wadell. © 1972. Used by permission of The University of Michigan Press.

Human beings: *Vatican Council II: The Conciliar and Post Conciliar Documents*, New Revised Edition Austin Flannery, OP, ed. © 1992, Costello Publishing Company, Inc. Used by permission of the publisher. All rights reserved.

You, neighbor God: *Poems from the Book of Hours* by Rainier Maria Rilke, tr. by Babette Deutch. © 1941, New Directions Publishing Corp. Used by permission of the publisher.

Somewhere in life: "Frail and Glorious" as specified from *A Tree Full of Angels* by Macrina Wiederkehr. © 1988, Macrina Wiederkehr. Reprinted by permission of HarperCollins Publishers, Inc.

The formidable: *Learning to Forgive* by Doris Donnelly. © 1979, Abingdon Press. Used by permission.

Let us pray: *A Christian's Prayer Book*, published by Franciscan Herald Press.

There are only: *The Great Divorce* by C.S. Lewis. Used by permission of HarperCollins, Ltd.

Once upon a time: *The Brothers Karamazov* by Fyodor Dostoevsky, trans. Constance Garnett, 1957.

When the sins: *Fences* by August Wilson. © 1986, August Wilson. Used by permission of Dutton Signet, a div. of Penguin Books USA Inc.

There is: "A Prayer for the Lady Who Forgave Us," (19) *The Hour of the Unexpected* by John Shea. © 1977, Tabor Publishing, a div. of RCL Enterprises.

A brother: *The Desert Fathers,* tr. from the Latin with an Introduction by Helen Wadell, © 1972. Used by permission of The University of Michigan Press.

Love is: "Love Is Not Concerned," *Horses Make a Landscape Look More Beautiful,* by Alice Walker. © 1984, Alice Walker. Used by permission of Harcourt Brace & Company.

In a divinized: *The Theologia Germanica of Martin Luther,* Bengt Hoffman, tr. © 1980, Paulist Press. Used by permission.

Human society: letter to Ernesto Cardenal "May 16, 1962" from *The Courage for Truth* by Thomas Merton. © 1993, Thomas Merton Legacy Trust.

One of the most: *Raids on the Unspeakable* by Thomas Merton. © 1966, Abbey of Gethsemani, Inc. Used by permission of New Directions Publishing Corp.

Sin is an unused: *Gravity and Grace* by Joseph Sittler, © 1986, Augsburg Publishing House. Used by permission of Augsburg Fortress.

I'll go no more: *The Complete Works of William Shakespeare,* revised edition, Hardin Craig and David Bevington, eds. © 1973, Scott Foresman & Company. Used with permission.

No matter: *Forgiveness* by Archbishop Daniel E. Pilarczyk, © 1992. Used by permission of Our Sunday Visitor.

You are the Devil: *The Name of the Rose* by Umberto Eco, © 1980, Gruppo Editoriale Fabbri-Bompiani, Sonzogno, Etas S.p.A., English tr. © 1983, Harcourt Brace & Company and Martin Secker & Warburg Limited. Used by permission of Harcourt Brace & Company.

I am not: letter to 'A.' "2 August 55," *The Habit of Being* by Flannery O'Connor, © 1979, Regina O'Connor. Used by permission of Farrar, Straus & Giroux, Inc.

Satan is: *Den of Lions* by Terry A. Anderson, © 1993, TMS Corporation. Used by permission of Crown Publishers, Inc.

(29) **Sin is present:** *The Humility of God* by John Macquarrie, © 1978, Westminster Press.

We raise de wheat: "Slave Song," *My Bondage and My Freedom* by Frederick Douglass. Used by permission of Dover Publications.

He was a bad Catholic: *The Heart of the Matter,* by Graham Greene. Viking Press.

My face is: "A Poem About Faith," *The Middle of the World* by Kathleen Norris, © 1981. Reprinted by permission of University of Pittsburgh Press.

I would like: *On Earth as in Heaven* by Dorothee Soelle, tr. Marc Batko, © 1993, Westminster Press.

Long ago: *The Mood of Christmas,* by Howard Thurman, © 1973, Howard Thurman.

Some say: "Fire and Ice," *The Poetry of Robert Frost,* Edward Connery Latham, ed. © 1951, Robert Frost. Copyright © 1923, 1969, Henry Holt & Co., Inc. Used by permission of Henry Holt & Co., Inc.

Your father: *Billy Phelan's Greatest Game* by William Kennedy. © 1978, William Kennedy. Used by permission of Viking Penguin, a div. of Penguin Books USA Inc.

I lost my soul: "Lost One Soul" by Sandy McIntosh from *Jamaica Woman,* Pamela Mordecai & Mervyn Morris, eds.

Foul whisp'rings: *The Complete Works of William* (40) *Shakespeare,* revised edition, Hardin Craig and David Bevington, eds., © 1973, Scott Foresman & Company. Used by permission.

Ethan went away: *The Accidental Tourist* by Anne Tyler. ©1985, Anne Tyler Modarressi. Used by permission of Alfred A. Knopf, Inc.

Young man: "The Prodigal Son," *God's Trombone,* by James Weldon Johnson. © 1927, The Viking Press, Inc., renewed © 1955, Grace Nail Johnson. Used by permission of Viking Penguin, a div. of Penguin USA Inc.

In confession: *Life Together* by Dietrich Bonhoeffer. English tr. © 1954, Harper & Brothers, © renewed 1982, Helen S. Doberstein.

My father: *The Stories of John Cheever* by John Cheever, © 1978. Used by permission of Alfred A. Knopf, Inc.

Suffering is: *Reconciliation: Mission and Ministry in a Changing Social Order* by Robert J. Schreiter, CPPS, in The Boston Theological Institute Series, vol. 3, 1992.

They tell us: "Scars," *An Oregon Message* by William Stafford. © 1987, William Stafford. Used by permission of HarperCollins Publishers, Inc.

When I first: *The Book of Qualities* by J. Ruth Gendler. © 1988, J. Ruth Gendler, HarperCollins Publishers. Used by permission.

Being human: *The Needs of Strangers* by Michael Ignatieff. © 1985, Michael Ignatieff. Used by permission of Viking Penguin, a div. of Penguin USA Inc.

One thing: *For Colored Girls Who Have Considered Suicide When the Rainbow Is Enuf* by Ntozake Shange. © 1975, 1976, 1977, Ntozake Shange. Used by permission of Simon & Schuster.

The outcast: *The Name of the Rose* by Umberto Eco, © 1980, Gruppo Editoriale Fabbri-Bompiani, Sonzogno, Etas S.p.A., English tr. © 1983, Harcourt Brace & Company and Martin Secker & Warburg

Limited. Used by permission of Harcourt Brace & Company.

Then my family: *The Prince of Tides* by Pat Conroy. © 1986, Pat Conroy. Used by permission of Houghton Mifflin Co. All rights reserved.

(50) **The legend:** "Shapeshifter Poems" by Lucille Clifton. From *The Language of Life: A Festival of Poets,* Bill Moyers and James Haba, eds., 1995. Published by Bantam Doubleday Dell.

Forgiveness is: *Markings* by Dag Hammarskjold, tr. Auden/Sjoberg. Tr. © 1964, Alfred A. Knopf, Inc. and Faber and Faber, Ltd. Used by permission of Alfred A. Knopf, Inc.

This is something: *Mother Teresa: In My Own Words,* Jose Luis Gonzalez-Balado, comp., © 1996. Used by permission of Liguori Publications.

The Church must be ever ready: *Hope and Suffering* by Desmond Tutu. Published by Skotaville Publishers, Johannesburg, South Africa.

O Infinite: *Prayers for a Planetary Pilgrim* by Edward Hays, © Forest of Peace Publishing, Inc., Leavenworth, Kansas.

We cannot afford: *Markings* by Dag Hammarskjold, tr. Auden/ Sjoberg. Tr. © 1964, Alfred A. Knopf, Inc. and Faber and Faber, Ltd. Used by permission of Alfred A. Knopf, Inc.

The spirit: *The Old Testament Pseudepigrapha* by James H. Charlesworth. © 1983, 1985, James H. Charlesworth. Used by permission of Doubleday, a division of Bantam Doubleday Dell Publishing Group, Inc.

We are reminded: from *The Centering Moment,* by Howard Thurman. © 1969, Howard Thurman.

There can be: *Creed and Personal Identity* by David B. Harned, © 1981, Fortress Press. Used by permission of Augsburg Fortress.

In confession: *Life Together* by Dietrich Bonhoeffer. English tr. © 1954, Harper & Brothers, © renewed 1982, Helen S. Doberstein.

For a scientist: *Young Men and Fire* by Norman Maclean, © 1992, The University of Chicago. All rights reserved.

Old paint on canvass: *Pentimento: A Book of Portraits* by Lillian Hellman. Little, Brown & Co.

Never shall I: *Night* by Elie Wiesel, tr. by Stella Rodway. © 1960, MacGibbon & Kee, renewed © 1988 by the Collins Publishing Group. Used by permission of Hill and Wang, a div. of Farrar, Straus & Giroux, Inc.

i am running: "i am running into a new year," by Lucille Clifton. © 1987, Lucille Clifton. Reprinted from *Good Woman: Poems and a Memoir 1969-1980* by permission of BOA Editions, Ltd.

We have: *Gates of Forgiveness,* © 1993, Central Con- (60) ference of American Rabbis. Used by permission.

Exterior penances: *The Spiritual Exercises of St. Ignatius: A Literal Translation and a Contemporary Reading,* David L. Fleming, SJ, © 1978. Used by permission of The Institute of Jesuit Sources, St. Louis, Missouri.

The abbot: *The Desert Fathers,* tr. from the Latin with an Introduction by Helen Wadell, © 1972. Used by permission of The University of Michigan Press.

Let the abbot: *The Rule of St. Benedict,* tr. Justin McCann. Used by permission of Sheed and Ward, Kansas City, Missouri.

While we are: *The Apostolic Fathers,* 2nd ed. 1992, published by Baker Book House.

Years and: "Querencia," *An Oregon Message* by William Stafford. © 1987, William Stafford. Used by permission of HarperCollins Publishers, Inc.

To trivialize: *Reconciliation: Mission and Ministry in a Changing Social Order* by Robert J. Schreiter, CPPS, in The Boston Theological Institute Series, vol. 3, 1992.

People who: *Anne Frank: The Diary of a Young Girl* by Anne Frank. © 1952, Otto H. Frank. Used by permission of Doubleday, a div. of Bantam Doubleday Dell Publishing Group, Inc.

That's why: *Rabbit Is Rich* by John Updike, © 1981. Used by permission of Alfred A. Knopf, Inc.

Remorse is: from *The Poems of Emily Dickinson,* Thomas H. Johnson, ed. Published by The Belknap Press of Harvard University Press, © 1951, 1955, 1979, 1983, President and Fellows of Harvard College. Used by permission of the publishers and Trustees of Amherst College.

What is there: "Lacrimae Amantis," *New and Collected Poems 1952-1992.* © 1994, Geoffrey Hill. Used by permission of Houghton Mifflin Co. All rights reserved.

Once a brother: *The Desert Fathers,* tr. from the Latin with an Introduction by Helen Wadell, © 1972. Used by permission of The University of Michigan Press.

What is needed: *An Interrupted Life* by Etty Hillesum, tr. by Arno Pomerans. English tr. © 1983, Jonathan Cape Ltd. © 1981, De Haan/Uniboek b.v., Bussum. Used by permission of Pantheon Books, a div. of Random House, Inc.

Behold I am: *The Old Testament Pseudepigrapha* by James H. Charlesworth. © 1983, 1985, James H. Charlesworth. Used by permission of Doubleday, a div. of Bantam Doubleday Dell Publishing Group, Inc.

All of ministry: *The Living Reminder* by Henri J. M. (69) Nouwen, © 1977. Published by Seabury Press.

Forgive us: *The Centering Moment,* by Howard Thurman, © 1969, Howard Thurman.

I shall now: *A Thousand Clowns* by Herb Gardner. © 1961, 1962, Herb Gardner and Irwin A. Cantor, Trustee. Used by permission of Random House, Inc.

Christ will come: *A Select Library of Nicene and Post-Nicene Fathers of the Christian Church,* © 1955. Used by permission of Wm. B. Eerdmans Publishing Co.

In a certain: *Tales of the Hasidim: The Early Masters,* by Martin Buber, tr. by Olga Marx. © 1947, 1948, © renewed 1975, Schocken Books, Inc. Used by permission of Schocken Books.

I detected: *The Comedians* by Graham Greene. Viking Press.

Let us review: *The Apostolic Fathers,* 2nd ed. 1992, published by Baker Book House.

(79) **And pray:** "Ash Wednesday" in *Collected Poems 1909–1962* by T.S. Eliot, © 1936, Harcourt Brace & Company, © 1964, 1963, T.S. Eliot, used by permission of the publisher.

We all have: *Gates of Forgiveness,* © 1993, Central Conference of American Rabbis. Used by permission.

[There are] two: *Old Age* by Helen M. Luke, © 1987. Used by permission of the Apple Farm Community.

Dear Lord God: *Luther's Prayers,* Herbert Brokering, ed., © 1994, Augsburg Fortress. Used by permission.

Let us repent by: *The Apostolic Fathers,* 2nd ed., 1992, published by Baker Book House.

Eternal God: *Gates of Forgiveness,* © 1993, Central Conference of American Rabbis. Used by permission.

Assuredly: *The Rule of Benedict* by Joan D. Chittister, OSB, © 1992. Used by permission of The Crossroad Publishing Co.

The act of: *Scenes of Clerical Life* by George Eliot. Published by Penguin USA Inc.

On Friday afternoon: "Pardon" *Various Miracles* by Carol Shields. © 1985, Carol Shields. Used by permission of Viking Penguin, a div. of Penguin USA Inc.

Now is: *Gates of Forgiveness,* © 1993, Central Conference of American Rabbis. Used by permission.

With you: *The Old Testament Pseudepigrapha* by James H. Charlesworth. © 1983, 1985, James H. Charlesworth. Used by permission of Doubleday, a div. of Bantam Doubleday Dell Publishing Group, Inc.

The new year: *African Religions: Symbol, Ritual, and Community* by Benjamin C. Ray, © 1976, Prentice-Hall, Inc. Used by permission.

To know: "Redeeming the Things We Can Never (90) Undo" by Paul J. Wadell. Previously published in *New Theology Review,* vol. 8:2. Used by permission of Paul J. Wadell.

The process: *Guilt and Healing* by Wilfred McGreal, © 1994. Used by permission of Geoffrey Chapman, an imprint of Cassell.

Each footstep: *Saint Maybe* by Anne Tyler, © 1991. Used by permission of Alfred A. Knopf, Inc.

Seven years ago: "Now or Never" *Bread and Roses,* by Astra. Virago Press.

To enter: *Reconciliation: Mission and Ministry in a Changing Social Order* by Robert J. Schreiter, CPPS. in The Boston Theological Institute Series, vol. 3, 1992.

Sin in human: *Penance: Reform Proposal for the Rite* by James Lopresti. Used by permission of James Lopresti.

I know too well: *Den of Lions* by Terry A. Anderson, © 1993, TMS Corporation. Used by permission of Crown Publishers, Inc.

It is a penance: *Dorothy Day: Selected Writings,* Robert Ellsberg ed., © 1983, 1992 by Robert Ellsberg and Tamar Hennessey. Published by Orbis Books.

In the Christian: *Theological Investigations* vol. XV by Karl Rahner, © 1982. Used by permission of The Crossroad Publishing Co.

Forgiveness breaks: *Markings* by Dag Hammarskjold, tr. Auden/Sjoberg. Tr. © 1964, Alfred A. Knopf, Inc. and Faber and Faber, Ltd. Used by permission of Alfred A. Knopf, Inc.

Those who: *Vatican Council II: The Conciliar and Post-Conciliar Documents,* New Rev. Edition, Austin Flannery, OP, ed., © 1992, Costello Publishing Company, Inc. Used by permission. All rights reserved.

Every endeavor to make peace: *Days of Devotion* by Pope John XXIII. © 1967, K. S. Giniger, Inc. Used by permission of Viking Penguin, a div. of Penguin Books USA Inc.

We owe it: *Learning to Forgive* by Doris Donnelly. © 1979, Abingdon Press. Used by permission.

Sin is a spreading: *Prayers for the Domestic Church* (100) by Edward Hays, © 1979, Forest of Peace Publishing, Inc., Leavenworth, Kansas.

Why is it: *Life Together* by Dietrich Bonhoeffer. English tr. © 1954, Harper & Brothers, © renewed 1982, Helen S. Doberstein.

This is the love: *Centering: In Pottery, Poetry and Person* by M. C. Richards. Wesleyan University Press.

The bloodied cross: "The Wine Cellar." Used by permission of the Society of the Precious Blood.

Reconciliation is: *Reconciliation: Mission and Ministry in a Changing Social Order* by Robert J. Schreiter, CPPS. In The Boston Theological Institute Series, vol. 3, 1992.

Human beings: *What is Psychoanalysis?* by D. W. Winnicott. Published by Bailliere, Tindall & Cassell, Ltd.

It would not be: *Catherine of Siena: The Dialogue,* Suzanne Noffke, OP, tr., © 1980, Paulist Press. Used with permission.

Lord, let me: *Gates of Forgiveness,* © 1993, Central Conference of American Rabbis. Used by permission.

By your cross: *Qurbono: The Book of Offering, Season of Great Lent and Passion Week,* Congregation Edition. ©1994, St. Maron Publications. Used by permission.

Forgiveness is: *Old Age* by Helen M. Luke, © 1987. Used by permission of the Apple Farm Community.

Where charity: Translated by Omar Westendorf, ©1960, World Library Publications, a division of J.S. Paluch Company, Inc. Schiller Park, Illinois. All rights reserved. Used by permission.

I am alone: *Selected Poetry of Jessica Powers,* Regina Siegfried, ASC and Robert F. Morneau, eds., © 1989. Used by permission of Sheed and Ward, Kansas City, Missouri.

(110) **A brother:** *The Desert Fathers,* tr. from the Latin with an Introduction by Helen Wadell, © 1972. Used by permission of The University of Michigan Press.

Christian reconciling: *Reconciled Sinners* by Dr. Bernard Cooke, © 1986.

Slowly turning: © 1993, Delores Dufner. Published by OCP Publications, Portland, Oregon. All rights reserved. Used by permission.

Convincing the world: *Crossing the Threshold of Hope* by His Holiness Pope John Paul II. Translation © 1994, Alfred A. Knopf, Inc. Used by permission of the publisher.

Give all people: *Prayers for a Lifetime* by Karl Rahner, © 1987. Used by permission of The Crossroad Publishing Co.

Never disappoint: *Rule for a New Brother,* tr. Benedictine Nuns of Cockfosters, © 1976. Used by permission of Templegate Publishers, Springfield, Illinois.

We have inherited: *The Living Reminder* by Henri J.M. Nouwen, © 1977. Published by Seabury Press.

What tasks: "The Wine Cellar." Used by permission of the Society of the Precious Blood.

Furthermore: *The Apostolic Fathers,* 2nd ed., 1992, published by Baker Book House.

You must: *Surprised by Joy, The Shape of My Early Life* by C.S. Lewis, © 1956, C.S. Lewis PTE Ltd., ©

renewed 1984, Arthur Barfield, used by permission of Harcourt Brace & Company.

The foundation: *Julian of Norwich: Showings,* Edmund Colledge, OSA, and James Walsh, SJ, tr., © 1978, Paulist Press. Used by permission.

I fear God: *Selected Poetry of Jessica Powers,* Regina Siegfried, ASC, and Robert F. Morneau, eds., © 1989. Used by permission of Sheed and Ward, Kansas City, Missouri.

Paul says rightly: "The Wine Cellar." Used by permission of the Society of the Precious Blood.

The literature: *Pilgrim at Tinker Creek* by Annie Dillard, © 1974. Published by Harper & Row.

It is not: *Seasons of Celebration* by Thomas Merton. (120) © 1965, the Abbey of Gethsemani. © renewed © 1993, Trustees of the Thomas Merton Legacy. Used by permission of Farrar, Straus & Giroux, Inc.

The quality of mercy: *The Merchant of Venice,* in *The Works of Shakespeare,* Sir Arthur Quiller-Couch and John Dover Wilson, eds. Used by permission of Cambridge University Press.

There is always: *A Raisin in the Sun* by Lorraine Hansberry. © 1988. Used by permission of Vintage Books, a subsidiary of Random House, Inc.

Let us be: *Strength to Love* by Martin Luther King, Jr. Published by Fortress Press.

An old man: *The Desert Fathers,* tr. from the Latin with an Introduction by Helen Wadell, © 1972. Used by permission of The University of Michigan Press.

Remind me: *Prayers for a Planetary Pilgrim* by Edward Hays, © Forest of Peace Publishing, Inc., Leavenworth, Kansas.

Two days later: *Song of Solomon* by Toni Morrison. © 1977, Alfred A. Knopf, Inc. Used by permission of International Creative Management, Inc.

There is one: *Holy the Firm* by Annie Dillard, © 1977. Published by Harper & Row.

God, again and again: *Rabindranath Tragore: Selected Poems,* tr. William Radice. Published by Penguin Ltd., London.

Forgiveness is: *Lenten Lunches: Reflections on the Weekday Readings for Lent and Easter Week,* © 1995, Daniel E. Pilarczyk. Reprinted by permission of St. Anthony Messenger Press, Cincinnati, Ohio. All rights reserved.

Compassion wears: *The Book of Qualities* by J. Ruth Gendler. © 1988, J. Ruth Gendler, HarperCollins Publishers. Used by permission.

Fridfeldt sat: *The Hammer of God* by Bo Giertz, © (130) 1960, 1973, Augsburg Publishing House. Used by permission of Augsburg Fortress.

I seek mercy: "For All Mary Magdalenes" by Desanka Maksimovic, tr. Vasa Mihailovich. Used by permission of Vasa Mihailovich

Come Lord: *An African Prayer Book* selected by Desmond Tutu. © 1995, Desmond Tutu. Used by permission of Doubleday, a div. of Bantam Doubleday Dell Publishing Group, Inc.

We like to: *The Gospel of God* by Anders Nygren, tr. L. J. Trinterud, © 1951, Westminster Press.

Without being: *The Human Condition* by Hannah Arendt, © 1958, The University of Chicago. All rights reserved.

For you are: *The Old Testament Pseudepigrapha* by James H. Charlesworth. © 1983, 1985, James H. Charlesworth. Used by permission of Doubleday, a div. of Bantam Doubleday Dell Publishing Group, Inc.

Lincoln tried love: *Strength to Love* by Martin Luther King, Jr. Published by Fortress Press.

I learned: *The Complete Poems of Patrick Kavanagh: with Commentary.* © 1996, Peter Kavanagh. Kavanagh Hand Press, Inc., New York.

Your mercy: *Gates of Forgiveness,* © 1993, Central Conference of American Rabbis. Used by permission.

The qualities: *Sin and Confession on the Eve of the Reformation* by Thomas N. Tentler.

Clearly, then: "Perspective on Sin" by William H. Shannon, in *The Priest,* 33:1, 1977. Used by permission of Our Sunday Visitor.

Don't carry: *Rule for a New Brother,* tr. Benedictine Nuns of Cockfosters, © 1976. Used by permission of Templegate Publishers, Springfield Illinois

(139) **Forgiveness:** *Meditations for the Passages and Celebrations of Life* by Noela E. Evans. Used by permission of Crown Publishers, Inc.

I once heard: *Lovingkindness: The Revolutionary Art of Happiness* by Sharon Salzberg, © 1995. Used by arrangement with Shambhala Publications, Inc., Boston.

Everyone says: *The Joyful Christian* by C.S. Lewis. Used by permission of HarperCollins, Ltd.

The biblical writers: *The Humility of God* by John Macquarrie, © 1978, Westminster Press.

Way back: *Atticus* by Ron Hansen. © 1996, Ron Hansen. Published by HarperCollins Publishers.

For a Catholic: *Den of Lions* by Terry A. Anderson, © 1993, TMS Corporation. Used by permission of Crown Publishers, Inc.

So, if I go: *St. Augustine: Confessions,* tr. R. S. Pine-Coffin. Published by Penguin Ltd., London.

Milly yearn[ed]: "Pardon," *Various Miracles* by Carol (150) Shields. © 1985, Carol Shields. Used by permission of Viking Penguin, a div. of Penguin USA Inc.

Rescue me: *The Old Testament Pseudepigrapha* by James H. Charlesworth. © 1983, 1985, James H. Charlesworth. Used by permission of Doubleday, a div. of Bantam Doubleday Dell Publishing Group, Inc.

I came to Mass: *The God Who Fell from Heaven* by John Shea. © 1992, John Shea. Used by permission of the publisher, Thomas More, Allen, Texas.

In our culture: *Holy Listening* by Margaret Guenther, © 1992. Used by permission of Cowley Publications, Boston.

The sixteenth-century: *Confession* by Max Thurian, © 1958. Published by SCM Press.

Just as baptism: *Summa Theologiae* by St. Thomas Aquinas. © Eyre & Spottiswode. Used by permission of Cambridge University Press.

The ministry: *Principles of Christian Theology* by John Macquarrie, © 1977, Charles Scribner's Sons. Used by permission.

They asked: *The Desert Fathers,* tr. from the Latin with an Introduction by Helen Wadell, © 1972. Used by permission of The University of Michigan Press.

Pore soul!: "Old Mrs. Harris," *Willa Cather's Collected Short Fiction, 1892-1912,* published by The University of Nebraska Press.

What, then: *A Select Library of Nicene and Post-Nicene Fathers of the Christian Church,* © 1955. Used with permission of Wm. B. Eerdmans Publishing Company.

There is a balm: *An African Prayer Book* selected by Desmond Tutu. © 1995, Desmond Tutu. Used by permission of Doubleday, a div. of Bantam Doubleday Dell Publishing Group, Inc.

Forgiveness is: *The Book of Qualities* by J. Ruth Gendler. © 1988, J. Ruth Gendler, HarperCollins Publishers. Used by permission.

We must: *Circles on the Water* by Marge Piercy. (160) ©1982, Marge Piercy. Used by permission of Alfred A. Knopf, Inc.

How do you: excerpt from *Women Who Run With the Wolves* by Clarissa Pinkola Estés, PHD, © 1992, 1995. All performance, derivative, adaptation, musical, audio, and recording, illustrative, theatrical, film, pictorial, electronic and all other rights reserved. Reprinted by permission of the author, Dr. Estés, and Ballantine Books, a div. of Random House, Inc.

Forgiveness is: *Putting Forgiveness Into Practice* by Doris Donnelly. © 1982, Tabor Publishing, a div. of RCL Enterprises.

In the last minutes: *Selected Poems 1966–1987* by Seamus Heaney. © 1990, Seamus Heaney. Used by permission of Farrar, Straus & Giroux, Inc., and Faber and Faber, Ltd.

The main question: "Sin and Reconciliation: Changing Attitudes in the Catholic Church" by Robert J. Hater. Originally printed in *Worship*, v. 59:1.

The sacrament: *The Rite of Penance: Commentaries*, vol. 3, Background and Directions, Nathan Mitchell, OSB, ed., © 1978 The Liturgical Conference. All rights reserved. Used by permission.

The highest: *Seasons of Celebration* by Thomas Merton. © 1965, Abbey of Gethsemani. © renewed 1993, Trustees of the Merton Legacy. Used by permission of Farrar, Straus & Giroux, Inc.

[T]he sacrament: *The Reconciling Community: The Rite of Penance* by James Dallen, © 1986. Used by permission of Pueblo Publishing.

In the cross: *The Rite of Penance: Commentaries*, vol. 3, Background and Directions, Nathan Mitchell, OSB, ed., © 1978, The Liturgical Conference. All rights reserved. Used with permission.

O God: *Medieval Handbooks of Penance*, John T. McNeill and Helena M. Gamer, eds. © 1938, 1990, Columbia University Press. Used by permission.

Dearly beloved: *Medieval Handbooks of Penance*, John T. McNeill and Helena M. Gamer, eds. © 1938, 1990, Columbia University Press. Used by permission.

(170) **After situating:** *Beloved* by Toni Morrison. © 1994, Alfred A. Knopf, Inc. Used by permission of International Creative Mgt., Inc.

Life drawn: *Rule for a New Brother*, tr. Benedictine Nuns of Cockfosters, © 1976. Used by permission of Templegate Publishers, Springfield, Illinois.

During his stay: *Tales of the Hasidim: The Early Masters* by Martin Buber, tr. Olga Marx. © 1947, 1948, © renewed 1975, Schocken Books, Inc. Used by permission of Schocken Books, distributed by Pantheon Books, a div. of Random House, Inc.

O mild Christ: "Feast Day," *The Lotus Flowers* by Ellen Bryant Voight. © 1987, Ellen Bryant Voight. Used by permission of W.W. Norton & Company, Inc.

Before sin: *Liturgy and Tradition: Theological Reflections of Alexander Schmemann*, Thomas Fisch, ed., © 1990. Used by permission of St. Vladimir's Seminary Press, Crestwood, New York.

Seventy times: *The God Who Fell from Heaven* by John Shea. © 1992, John Shea. Used by permission of Thomas More, Allen, Texas.

I'd love to: *My Mortal Enemy* by Willa Cather, © 1926. Used by permission of Alfred A. Knopf, Inc.

Out of what door: *Selected Poetry of Jessica Powers*, Regina Siegfried, ASC, and Robert F. Morneau, eds. © 1989. Used by permission of Sheed and Ward, Kansas City, Missouri.

And we sinners: *Symbol and Sacrament* by Michael Lawler, © 1987, Paulist Press. Used with permission.

Never be misled: *Rule for a New Brother*, tr. Benedictine Nuns of Cockfosters, © 1976. Used by permission of Templegate Publishers, Springfield, Illinois.

We cry: *Gates of Forgiveness*, © 1993, Central Conference of American Rabbis. Used by permission.   (180)

Yes to one: *Selected Poetry of Jessica Powers*, Regina Siegfried, ASC and Robert F. Morneau, eds. © 1989. Reprinted by permission of Sheed and Ward, Kansas City, Missouri.

A changed way: "Redeeming the Things We Can Never Undo" by Paul J. Wadell. Previously published in *New Theology* Review, v.8:2. Used by permission of Paul J. Wadell.

We struggled: *An African Prayer Book* selected by Desmond Tutu. © 1995, Desmond Tutu. Used by permission of Doubleday, a div. of Bantam Doubleday Dell Publishing Group, Inc.

The green: "spring song," by Lucille Clifton. © 1987, Lucille Clifton. *Good Woman: Poems and a Memoir 1969–1980*. Used by permission of BOA Editions, Ltd.

Mothering Presence: *Gates of Forgiveness*, © 1993, Central Conference of American Rabbis. Used by permission.

They had not the language: *The Descent of the Dove*, by Charles Williams. Published by The Religious Book Club, London.

The prophet: *Johannes Tauler: Sermons*, Maria Shrady, tr., © 1985, Paulist Press. Used by permission.

God's act: *The Rite of Penance: Commentaries*, vol. 3, Background and Directions, Nathan Mitchell, OSB, ed., © 1978, The Liturgical Conference. All rights reserved. Used by permission.

Come, you who: *Qurbono: The Book of Offering*, *Season of Great Lent and Passion Week*. © 1994, St. Maron Publications. Used by permission.   (190)

That's the difficulty: *Anne Frank: The Diary of a Young Girl* by Anne Frank. © 1952, Otto H. Frank. Used by permission of Doubleday, a div. of Bantam Doubleday Dell Publishing Group, Inc.

Looking down: "Good Night Willie Lee, I'll See You in the Morning," © 1975, Alice Walker (first appeared in the *Iowa Review*). *Good Night Willie Lee, I'll See You in the Morning* by Alice Walker. Used by permission of Doubleday, a div. of Bantam Doubleday Dell Publishing Group, Inc.

This is how: *In Memory of Her* by Elisabeth Schussler Fiorenza. Used by permission of The Crossroad Publishing Company

There are many: *Christopher Blumhardt and His Message* by R. Lejeune, © 1963, Plough Publishing House, Farmington, Pennsylvania. Used by permission.

I like the game: *All I Really Need to Know I Learned in Kindergarten* by Robert Fulghum, © 1988. Used by permission of Villard Books, a subsidiary of Random House, Inc.

Finding ourselves: *Dance of the Spirit* by Maria Harris. © 1989, Maria Harris. Used by permission of Bantam Books, a div. of Bantam Doubleday Dell Publishers Group, Inc.

All my life I: *The Color Purple* by Alice Walker. Published by Harcourt Brace.

The tradition: *The Reconciling Community: The Rite of Penance* by James Dallen, © 1986, Pueblo Publishing. Used by permission.

I am a frayed: *Pilgrim at Tinker Creek* by Annie Dillard, © 1974. Published by Harper & Row.

I shall die: "Conscientious Objector" by Edna St. Vincent Millay. From *Collected Poems,* Harper-Collins. © 1934, 1962, Edna St. Vincent Millay and Norma Millay Ellis. All rights reserved. Used by permission of Elizabeth Barnett, literary executor.

And then: "Merger Poem" by Judy Chicago. © 1979, Judy Chicago.

Author/Source Index